WITH MALICE TOWARDS SOME

TALES FROM A LIFE DANCING WITH STARS

BY

ROBERT SIDNEY

Bob Sidney (signature)

ISBN: 1-4107-3299-1 (e-book)
ISBN: 1-4107-3298-3 (Paperback)

This book is printed on acid free paper.

1stBooks - rev. 06/24/03

BOB SIDNEY'S CREDITS

TELEVISION SERIES:

Olsen & Johnson Hour (1949)
James Melton Hour
Four Star/All Star Review Theater
The Milton Berle Show
Dean Martin Show (1966-69)
Dean Martin Summer Show with
    Rowan & Martin (1967)
Dean Martin Golddiggers Show (1968)
Danny Thomas Review (1967-68)
Goldie/The Betty Hutton Show
    (1959-60)
Pearl Bailey Show (1971)
Dom DeLuise Show (1987-88)

TELEVISION SPECIALS:

Irving Berlin's Salute to America
    (1951) (NBC)
Academy Awards® Show (1957, 1958
    and 1966)
I'm Just Wild About Harry (CBS) -
    Betty Grable and Harry James –
    first television colorcast
Betty Hutton & Nat King Cole (1959)
That's My Mom (Pilot) starring Betty
    Hutton (1959)
Jack Benny (1959)
Hollywood Palace (1964-70)
Ed Sullivan Show (1964)
Tennessee Ernie Ford's Country
    Special (1968)
Roberta, starring Bob Hope (1969)
Bing Crosby and Friends (1974)
Bing Crosby and Family – 3 Christmas
    specials (1971-1973)
Perry Como – 2 Christmas specials
Mitzi Gaynor – The First Time (1973)
Red Hot Scandals of 1926 Parts 1 and
    II (1972, 1973) (NBC)
Dom DeLuise and Friends (1983-
    1986)

MOTION PICTURES:

This Is The Army (1943)
The Loves of Carmen (1948)
Slightly French (1949)
Bloodhounds on Broadway (1952)
Jumping Jacks (1952)
Susan Slept Here (1954)
The Conqueror (1956)
The Opposite Sex (1956)
You Can't Run Away From It (1956)
Party Girl (1958)
Where the Boys Are (1960)
How the West Was Won (1962)
Looking for Love (1964)
The Pleasure Seekers (1964)
How to Murder Your Wife (1965)
The Singing Nun (1965)
The Silencers (1966)
Valley of the Dolls (1967)

NIGHTCLUB ACTS

Betty Hutton
Debbie Reynolds
Mitzi Gaynor
Cyd Charisse and Tony Martin
Joey Heatherton
Bing Crosby and Friends

GALAS AND EXTRAVAGANZAS

Canadian National Exhibition
Sonja Henie Ice Show
Motion Picture Relief Gala honoring
    Frank Sinatra
Los Angeles Birthday Celebration

WITH MALICE TOWARDS SOME

What the stars say about working with Bob Sidney:

"With eternal gratitude." *Bing Crosby*

"Bob Sidney was my favorite teacher. He taught me lessons I value and use to this day. He is a brilliant man; but most of all he is my friend." *Debbie Reynolds*

"It is not often you get to work with someone as talented as Bob Sidney. I love him." *June Allyson*

"I am so privileged to have worked with Bob Sidney and am so grateful for his love and friendship." *Mitzi Gaynor*

"I learned so much from working with Bob Sidney. He is brilliantly talented and wickedly funny." *Florence Henderson*

"Bob shows great taste in everything he does." *Tony Martin*

"Working with Bob is great fun, yet very, very productive."
Cyd Charisse

"What I know about 'working' a stage I learned from Bob Sidney. I consider him my teacher and my friend."
Frank Sinatra, Jr.

"I cherish the sweet memories that I have working with Bob Sidney. It was truly a pleasure and I thank him for it."
Ann-Margret

"Working for 12 years with Dean Martin was greatly enhanced by Bob Sidney and his amazing barrel of monkeys." *Dom DeLuise*

Acknowledgments

I gratefully acknowledge the following people for their assistance: Jeff Teich, Sue Berger Ramin, Joni Berry, Joe Tremaine, Neil Daniels, Sue Kelly, Larry Billman, Lee Hale, Kate Kahn, Joel Coleman, Michael Rowe and Madame Fenya Merksaeme.

CONTENTS

Foreword

WITH MALICE TOWARDS SOME is a compilation of vignettes of personalities whom I have worked with. There is a vast cast of characters from television, films, theatre, opera, and public life. I have tried to avoid the practice of the biographer who writes intimate stories about people he has never known or even met. Most of my stories, I hope, will be new and fresh about celebrities we revered as role models or icons.

I have refrained from writing an autobiography, as I am afraid that I will be arrested for having written my life's story, and jailed for having lived it.

I dedicate this to my father, who always wanted me to be a writer. I hope that perhaps, someday, I will be.

Robert Sidney

Introduction

The first time I saw a dancer execute a cartwheel, I was so impressed I announced "I am going to be a dancer when I grow up." The first time I saw a tightrope walker perform in a circus, I decided that when I grew up I was going to be a tightrope walker. I forgot all about dancing. I was so excited about that adventure that some of my friends and I found a big old rope in the garage. We attached one end to an elm tree and the other end to one of the eaves of my house. It was quite taut and with umbrella in hand, I did my tightrope-walking act. With my first step out onto the rope, I fell and broke my ankle. I knew right then and there that I was destined to be a dancer.

Curiously enough, when my ankle healed I did study dancing at the local dancing school. I managed to learn a few things, especially from a girl next door who was a very advanced student and a good friend of mine. She would teach me some of the advanced steps that she had learned. High school was very uneventful. I appeared in a play occasionally; however, I was too preoccupied dealing with the agonies of adolescence.

My career started to take shape when I got to college. I enrolled in New York University, not because of its academia, but because it was so close to Broadway – the Valhalla of Show Business. Actually, my major in college was Political Science. In fact, I got a working scholarship in that department. But I spent most of my time with the Dramatic Society, appearing in the plays or directing some of them. Working on the Varsity shows – they were always musicals - was exciting, because I could stage some numbers now and then. But I always managed to get uptown and take a class with an important dancing teacher. The students up there were actually professional dancers who came to class to keep in condition. So I was exposed to that environment of professionalism.

During summer holidays, I would work in summer stock, if I could get a job, or else I would work in one of the summer resorts that had an entertainment staff. It paid well, and also kept me busy in the business I liked.

After college, I auditioned for a musical called *On Your Toes* and was accepted. I was even given a small part. I was very excited because the choreographer of *On Your Toes* was the maestro George Balanchine. After *On Your Toes*, a friend of mine hired me for a play he was directing by Richard Maibaum called *Birthright*. Although the play was a good one and its anti-Nazi message was important, nobody seemed to worry too much about Hitler until he actually marched into Poland. So the play didn't have a very long run, but I had a good credit for my resume as "Stage Manager."

After the show closed, I got a part and danced in *Keep off the Grass*. Here again, Balanchine was the choreographer of the show. People thought I was his assistant because I was always by his side. He had difficulty speaking English, so he would tell me things in French and I would translate for him. So he insisted that I stay close to him; and in effect I really was his assistant, albeit an unpaid one.

After that, I went out with the touring company of *I Married an Angel*, another show that Balanchine had choreographed. I had a dancing role and understudied Burl Ives. I got to know the star of the show, Vivienne Segal, and we became very dear friends and remained so until she died. As for Burl Ives, he went on a drunk when we arrived in California, so I went on for him and took his role for the duration of the run.

I then got a job as Assistant Stage Manager for a musical called *Banjo Eyes*, which starred Eddie Cantor. We had beautiful showgirls in it. (One of them was Jacqueline Susann, who later wrote the novel *Valley of the Dolls*, the movie version of which I coincidentally staged.) My job was to supervise the dancers and keep the dance numbers in shape. When we were on the road with the show before we came to Broadway, I had to re-do some of the numbers. My reward was recognition by Hassard Short, the producer of the show. Hassard was also the producer of Irving Berlin's *Music Box Reviews* and one of his closest friends.

When Irving Berlin had just finished writing his legendary all-soldiers show *This Is The Army*, he complained to Hassard that he needed a choreographer and where would he find one that was a soldier in the Army? Hassard said "they just drafted Bob Sidney and he'll do the job for you." I was a foot soldier in the Army, until Irving Berlin had me transferred to the "This Is The Army" outfit. I choreographed and staged the musical numbers for *This Is The Army*, and performed the same duties for the Warner Brothers film version of the show, in which Ronald Reagan played one of the leading roles. So I guess it can be said that the Second World War helped launch my career immeasurably.

After the War, Columbia Pictures signed me to a term contract as choreographer, where I got to work with my idol, Rita Hayworth. From then on it was relatively clear sailing. On Broadway, I staged and choreographed *Three to Make Ready*, *Along Fifth Avenue* and several other shows. In Hollywood, I worked on *Where the Boys Are*, *How the West Was Won*, *Valley of the Dolls*, *The Opposite Sex* and some twelve other films.

In between all this activity, I staged nightclub acts for Bing Crosby and Family, Mitzi Gaynor, Cyd Charisse and Tony Martin, Betty Hutton, Debbie Reynolds and Joey Heatherton. I was very flattered when asked to stage several of the Academy Award® shows, and particularly pleased to co-produce one of them with Joe Pasternak.

I have over 200 hours in prime time television to my credit. Some of the shows involved were *The Milton Berle Show*, *The Pearl Bailey Show*, *The Betty Hutton Show*, *The Four Star Review*, *The Danny Thomas Review and The James Melton Hour*. I also staged all of Bing Crosby's and Perry Como's Christmas shows and many other television specials. I spent some four years choreographing the highly successful Dean Martin television show and three years directing and choreographing the Dean Martin Golddiggers' show.

Although I am retired now, I am still dedicated to the welfare of the dancer. I am the Chairman of the Advisory Board of the Professional Dancers Society, an affiliate of the Actors Fund of America. In my book, *With Malice Towards Some: Tales from a Life Dancing With Stars*, I have tried to reflect back on my long career and remember some of the superstars who filled my life with excitement, satisfaction and gratitude.

This Is The Army

The United States had no sooner entered the Second World War, when General Marshall, the Army Chief of Staff in Washington, asked Irving Berlin to write another soldier show, just as he had done during the First World War. At that time, Irving Berlin wrote a modest but very effective army show called *Yip, Yip, Yaphank*. It did much for the morale of our country and our troops. Irving Berlin was in the middle of a very important project in Hollywood. He was working on a musical film called *Holiday Inn* with Bing Crosby and Fred Astaire. When General Marshall made his request, Irving Berlin immediately put his duties on the film on hold and started work on a new Army show that he called *This Is The Army*. Once it was finished, some 300 of us soldiers who had been in show business in civilian life were drafted from different branches of the service and were all convened at Camp Upton, where rehearsals started. When we weren't rehearsing, we went on with our Army duties.

The show opened on Broadway on Independence Day, July 4th, 1942. Never in the history of Broadway had an opening night been so electrifying. It was the #1 Box Office hit on Broadway. Since the proceeds from the show went to Army Relief and the morale factor of the show made its mark immediately, the show had an incredible run on Broadway.

After Broadway, we went to Washington for a special performance for President Franklin Delano Roosevelt and the members of the government who were fortunate enough to get a seat for the show. On opening night, when we arrived at the theatre, we were examined very closely by the Secret Service. When they were finished, the FBI had a go at us. Even backstage, on a catwalk – the area way above the rig that holds the lights – there were two FBI agents with big 45 caliber guns pointed at the stage in case something went awry. The show was received as enthusiastically as it had been on Broadway. We were invited back to the White House, and each one of us was introduced to the President and then to the First Lady, Eleanor Roosevelt. That charming lady – a wonderful charismatic person – was so interested in us that she took us on a tour of some of the most important rooms. She made us

1

feel completely at home. Her enthusiasm made the Washington experience a lasting memory.

The first act finale was a number Mr. Berlin wrote called *A Soldier's Dream*, featuring pretty waitresses serving breakfast in bed to a GI. The waitresses were, of course, boys in drag and they really weren't very pretty. The "dream girls" were Gene Nelson, Richard Irving, Joe Johnston and myself, "We Hairy Legged Lovelies." The number ended hilariously and closed the first act. I was on my way to my dressing room when someone said Mr. Berlin wanted to see me immediately. I arrived at his room still wearing my drag costume, which was now half way off my body. He introduced me to a visitor, Evelyn Walsh MacLean, the owner of the ill-fated, legendary Hope Diamond. She was wearing it and a bodyguard stood close by to make sure no one stole it. She had seen the show twice and wanted to see it again, but no seats were available, so her dear friend Irving invited her to watch the show from backstage.

When she saw me dressed as a girl, she asked, "Why don't you wear this?" and threw the famous bauble at me. "But I must warn you," she added, "there is a curse attached to it and anyone who even touches it ends up in a tragedy." I told her that I would take my chances. I wasn't uneasy about the curse. I'm insensitive to superstition. As I started to put on the incredibly huge blue diamond, which was attached to a string of fairly good white diamonds, her bodyguard said, "I'm sorry, Mrs. MacLean, he'll have to give it back to you. That's one of the conditions of the insurance company." The Hope Diamond is now in the Smithsonian Museum in Washington, and my claim to fame is that I had it first in my own hands a short while before they ever got a hold of it and put it on display for thousands of people to admire. As for the legendary curse, all I can say is that sixty years after I held it in my hands, I'm still here.

From Washington, we toured every major city and finally ended in Hollywood to do the film version of *This Is The Army*. We rehearsed at the Warner Brothers Studios daily. Most of us had to hitch a ride to get to the studio. I was once thumbing it, when this expensive Cadillac picked me up. When I got in the car, the man driving asked me where I was going and I told him down the hill to Warner Brothers. He said, "Oh, you must be one of the soldiers working on the show there." And I said, "Yes, I am." He asked what I thought of Warner Brothers. I told him, "Everybody is so very nice there. They really have been very kind to us. We love it." Then he asked, "What do you hear about Jack Warner?" I said, "Everyone says he's a son of a bitch." Well, we kept chatting and came to the bottom of the hill, and then he started to drive through the gates of the Studio. I said, "No, no, no, you can't do that. Let me off here. I'll get in trouble if you go through the gates." He said, "Now, look. Don't worry, I can go through those gates if I want to. I'm Jack Warner."

The Warner Brothers' film version of *This Is The Army* was quite different from what we did in the theatre. In the stage version, we did a good musical review with one number after the other. Hollywood changed that. The writers at Warner Brothers came up with a story about this young officer going off to war, leaving his best girl and his mother. It was a real flag-waving scenario. The part of the young soldier was played by a lieutenant in the Army named Ronald Reagan. Of course, he never went off to war. He just went off to the nearest special service outfit where he remained throughout the war. I had the privilege and honor to stage and choreograph *This Is The Army* on stage; and I was asked to do the same for the film version. The numbers I staged on Broadway took on a new dimension in Hollywood. For example, in our stage version on Broadway we used two hundred soldiers. In the film version, we used a thousand. We borrowed most of these men from nearby Army bases. It wasn't easy getting these men to do complicated Army drill to music. They had never done that before. However, fortunately, some of the men in our outfit helped me. We each would get groups and teach them the number. It did turn out amazingly well. On Broadway we also performed Irving Berlin's *How About a Cheer for the Navy*. On stage, a hundred and fifty of us dressed as sailors performed the number. In Hollywood, they had a wonderful mock-up of a real battleship and we had six hundred Army men dressed as sailors performing the number. Someone gave me the bright idea at the very end to spell out "Navy" in semaphores, which is the art of conveying messages using flags. For each letter of the alphabet, there is a movement with a flag. I chose the ones that I thought were most effective, and I used my own design in creating this part of the show. However, I didn't spell out the four-letter word "N-A-V-Y" as I intended. Instead, I spelled out a well-known four-letter word that got your mouth washed out with soap if you used it as a kid. Fortunately, a naval officer who was a guest at the shoot stopped the cameras and explained to us why we couldn't do it. I was very grateful to him, because if this had been discovered by anyone watching or someone at Warner Brothers, I would still be in the brig.

There's a sequence in the film which depicts the members of the cast and the various branches of the Army from which they were recruited, such as Infantry, Artillery, Signal Corps, Medics and so on. Michael Curtiz, the director, was elated when he was informed that the War Department had given Warner Brothers permission to use Camp Roberts, a training center for the Army Tank Division, because he thought it would add color to see someone in a tank being drafted for the show. Since we had no one in our outfit who had been in the Tank Division, he said they would use me as the draftee for that sequence.

I was delighted. We went up on location to Camp Roberts, where the Commanding Officer wasn't too excited about the invasion of his Camp by Hollywood. He was very firm and notified Michael Curtiz that we could have only one shot in getting what we wanted, and then "Out!"

Curtiz was in a quandary, and we finally decided that we could get two chairs and simulate a tank. I was to sit in one seat and the driver in the other, and rehearse our commands as they were given to us. When Curtiz yelled "Action!" I was to grab the driver's thigh very firmly, and at the next command, press even harder on his thigh, which meant "Get to a speed of about 20 miles per hour." The next command would be to relax my grip a bit, so the tank would slow down and they could get a close-up of me being notified that I was being drafted for "This Is The Army".

Next, the command would be to grab the driver's thigh firmly again, so he could resume speed. The final command would be "Cut!" which meant I would relax my grip, take my hand off his thigh, and the tank would come to a halt.

We went over this four or five times and we thought we were letter-perfect. It was time to shoot the scene, so the driver and I took our positions in the tank. Curtiz yelled "Action!"

I went to grab the driver's thigh. I didn't realize that there was a perpendicular post in the tank between the two of us, and it was impossible to get my hand around it. When I grabbed what I thought was his thigh, I had to reach higher up and got a fistful of the family jewels.

I held on and wouldn't let go, because I remembered the admonition from the post commander who said we had only one try at the scene. If I took my hand off, that would be the cue for driver to stop the tank, and if he did, that would be the end of the shot and we would all be sent off the base.

It was a difficult situation for me, and the constant up-and-down, up-and-down motion on that bumpy road didn't help either. In fact, it only accentuated the problem in hand.

The next command was to "Increase Speed," and I grabbed more firmly and held on. The command came to "Slow Up," so they could get a close-up of me being drafted for the show. I was laughing uncontrollably when the camera came in on me. But I never let go.

The command came to "Increase Speed," again. Curtiz depended on me to make this scene work, and I was determined that it would. I held on for dear life.

The final command was "Stop," which meant I could release my hold on this poor driver.

So ended this non-scheduled, impromptu "Treat Your Tank Buddy to a Helping Hand Day." The production staff was happy because we got it all in one take. But Michael Curtiz was swearing in Hungarian. I knew he was upset with someone. I didn't realize he was angry with me.

"Vat was so funny that you laugh?" Before I could explain what happened, he went at the poor, blushing tank driver, and said to him, "And you! Don't try. Don't even try. An actor you will never be. You don't know how to control emotions."

When we finished the film at Warner Brothers, we traveled back east, because *This Is The Army* was to go overseas. 150 men were chosen

5

to become the overseas outfit. I had something to do with the selection of the men, because it meant staging new numbers in the overseas version. Those of us who were chosen to go overseas were very proud. We couldn't wait to do our jobs. The Army had a problem, though. It had been announced in Washington that no soldier would go overseas unless he had basic training. Most of us did not have basic training. And so, to accomplish this, they took us out to a rifle range in New Jersey someplace, handed each one of us a Carbine-22 and told us to shoot at a target. Well, it was mayhem. It was a danger zone, definitely. Most of our guys had never held a rifle in their hands. They shot at everything but the targets. It was a risky business to be in that area. But somehow we survived; they called it basic training, and the next thing we knew we were on the ship The Queen Mary, going to England.

We arrived in Liverpool and we were put on a train and got off in London, carrying two barracks packs on our shoulders. One of our officers insisted that we must act like soldiers, and so we shouted as we walked down the streets, "Hut, two. Hut, two. Hut, two." When suddenly, we heard our first air raid siren. Automatically to a man, our shout went to a whisper. We even walked on our toes, thinking the enemy wouldn't hear us. And then the bomb dropped. That was our introduction to nightlife in London. We got to the Palladium Theatre and spent two days there, hardly leaving it because there was so much work to do. The new version for 150 men rather than the 300 we were accustomed to required many changes. I had to do them in record time. But we got the show on and our opening night was very impressive. Whoever said that the English are very reserved was not at the theatre that night. They cheered, they hooted, they stomped so loudly you couldn't hear the air raid sirens, and when you could hear them they stayed in their seats and did not seek refuge in the air raid shelters. Strangely enough, they never did leave. They watched the show and were very intrigued by it.

We had all sorts of dignitaries come and see the show: the King and Queen, Princess Elizabeth (now Queen Elizabeth) and Princess Margaret, Five-Star Generals, Naval Aristocracy, Crowned Heads of Europe. In fact, if we ever finished a performance and someone below the rank of Brigadier General came back stage after the show to salute us, we were slightly offended. One night, I was about to make my entrance in a number when I noted a strange array of people. It was a middle-aged woman and she had teenagers with her. And they all had hatchets and things like that in their hands. I turned to one of the stagehands and asked what those people over there were about. He said, "That's the detonation squad. There's a bomb supposedly on top of this theatre and they're going up to detonate it." And then, with that, it was time to make my entrance. Throughout the number, I kept thinking, "Any moment now. Any moment now." But the moment did not happen. And it did do one thing for me. From that time on, I never ever was concerned about an air raid. My respect for the English grew immeasurably. I admired their courage and determination during the War. I became an Anglophile and I still am.

After London, we did a tour of all the major British cities. As with everywhere else, we did much for the morale of our troops and the English citizens. We also raised millions of pounds for British war charities. When we got back to London, we had ended our tour of England. The Special Service officers, even though they had nothing to do with the show's production, had taken all the bows and credit for this unusual theatrical event. It was their suggestion to the military that the show be disbanded after its run ended. They further recommended that the cast be assigned to regular military outfits. After all, we were basically soldiers first who also happened to be performers. We would have stood a better chance for survival if we had been shipped directly to one of Hitler's concentration camps than be assigned to a U.S. fighting outfit. They were trained to fight. We weren't. That fiasco at the rifle range in the States was the only training we ever had. We still had greasepaint behind our ears.

And now that *This Is The Army* had served its purpose, it would be disbanded, or so Special Services thought. Some of us knew the right people in London, namely Binkie Beaumont, the head of H.M. Tenant Ltd., the most important theatrical production company in the West End. We told Binkie our problem and he promised he would take care of it. He did. He invited an old buddy, General Montgomery, the commander-in-chief of the British Forces, to the Palladium to see a performance of the show. It took little pressure to sell Monty the idea of borrowing *This Is The Army*, now that it was up for grabs, from the U.S. Army to entertain British troops. Monty had an old score to settle with Dwight D. Eisenhower. He felt he should have been chosen as Supreme Allied Commander, not Eisenhower. By annexing the U.S. Army show, it would be a tactical victory of sorts. However, when Eisenhower was asked to approve this unusual request, he announced he would see the show first before he made his decision.

After the curtain came down, we were called to attention as the very impressive general appeared. He ordered us at ease and announced the show would not be disbanded; on the contrary, we were to remain the This Is The Army detachment under his command. He told us how much the show would mean to American troops. It would remind them of home just as it did him. We were to travel and perform wherever there was an American G.I. He told us to prepare for hardships along the way that would make the air raids in London a piece of cake. He impressed upon us that we were soldiers with a very important mission, we were the morale builders for our fighting men. General Eisenhower visited us and touched our lives that day. He was the first ranking American officer overseas who recognized and appreciated the contribution made to the war effort by Irving Berlin's *This Is The Army*.

We were on our way to join the Fifth Army in Italy! Our boat, fortunately, could travel faster than 35 knots per hour. On our way down to Naples, we outran a submarine and even dodged its torpedo. Naples was a bombed-out harbor, ships turned upside down. It was really desolate – a very eerie site. We were booked in the Royal Palace, but only because it was being used by troops there. There was no roof to the place. And that's where they put us. The British anti-aircraft force was on the level below us, and below them were Italian prisoners of war. The first night we got there, we were introduced to what they called a local air raid. Because compared to the English raids, that air raid was really tepid.

We were to open *This Is The Army* at the Opera House in Naples. We had two days in which to make adjustments to their stage. I had posted on our billboard a rehearsal schedule for the show. When I got there I was surprised to see that someone had changed it. I asked, "Who did this?" One of our officers said, "I did." It was my duty to remind him that we had officers only as figureheads because we were an outfit and every American company had to have officers. Otherwise, our so-called officers had nothing to do with the show but just enjoy its benefits. I told him that we were going to rehearse according to the schedule I had announced. And he said, "No you're not. You're going to do it my way."

I said, "Up yours." And with that, he said, "You're confined to quarters, Sergeant Robert Sidney." I had to go back to my quarters and he, in turn, went to the local commanding officer and reported my insubordination. What he didn't realize at the time was that insubordination in a war area to an officer was punishable by death. I was in a serious position. But luck was with me, because Irving Berlin decided at the last moment in Hollywood that he was going to be present at the opening in Naples. He arrived the day before we were to open our show. He asked our First Sergeant Alan Anderson where I was. Alan explained to him my predicament. Irving said, "What do you mean he's being court-marshaled? We have no time for court-marshals. We have a show to do." He actually went to the local commanding officer and presented his case. The officer made a great mistake. He told Irving Berlin, "This is a military matter and you're a civilian, so I suggest you butt out." Very wrong thing to say to Irving Berlin, because he called General Marshall in Washington directly and within ten minutes after his call, this officer was told exactly what to do and the show went on. To this day, I am grateful to Irving Berlin because he saved my neck – literally.

In any event, the show as usual did very well. The troops enjoyed it. Irving Berlin left for the States and his movie, *Holiday Inn*, from which he kept leaving to make sure we were okay. We went on to a little town called Santa Maria. We had a shortened version of the show with a smaller unit so that we could play in smaller venues like a military hospital or an open field. Santa Maria was more or less where American troops came off the front line and had a day or two off from the fighting. They enjoyed our show as much as did the people in the big theatres. While in Santa Maria, one of our soldiers, Ross Elliot, found a stray dog. It became his pet. We christened the dog "Tita" after "This Is The Army". The dog didn't care much for us, but it never left Ross' side and was able to travel with him throughout Italy because we were transported on jeeps and trucks.

From there we went to Bagnoli, which was Mussolini's recreation center for his troops. Once again, they put us on top of this building that had been bombed out. That very night when we first arrived in Bagnoli, Mount Vesuvius was erupting. It was a startling sight to see all this red molten lava shoot into the sky. Suddenly, German airplanes appeared overhead, decided to counterattack and get Naples back.

Anything that could fly was in that sky, and our anti-aircraft guns were firing away. It was quite a sight to see the red of the molten lava and the red of the man-made tracer bullets. I was assigned to act as air-raid warden wherever we were, and I made sure our guys got indoors during the attack. However, Joe Fretwell, who was the costume designer, was out on this little parapet, watching this display of Vesuvius and our artillery firing at planes overhead. I said, "Come inside Joe, I order you to come inside." He replied, "Oh stop all that nonsense. Come here and tell me what you think. Which is more startling: The red of Vesuvius or the red of the tracer bullets?" Just then, a two-seater Fokker plane with the biggest swastika painted on it came diving down at us and was strafing us with bullets. And Joe looked at this plane with the big swastika and said, "Aren't our boys brave?" With that I looked up and said, "Nobody will ever get us. We're immune to air raids."

We then left in convoy jeeps they assigned to us and were on our way to Rome. We had our orders for where we were to stay. As we drove over the mountains and hills through these little towns, you knew people were behind us drawing shutters. You could almost hear the whispers, yet there wasn't a sign of life. When we got to Rome, we found our little hotel, which, as usual, was a bombed out building. We could hear artillery fire in the distance. We made ourselves at home among the cement, which we slept on. And after our second day there, one of our non-coms went out and reported to headquarters. He announced, "This Is The Army detachment reporting for duty." The officer asked, "When did you get here?" He answered, "Two days ago." The officer told him, "You couldn't have. We only took Rome this morning."

Our show in Rome played mostly to American troops and some British troops as well. It met with great approval. The Vatican invited us to an audience with the Pope. It meant so much to the Catholic members of our troop and many of the non-Catholics. There's something about the Vatican that really makes you meditate. It's very inviting and we really had been through too much activity. We left Italy and there again did so much for the morale of our troops and the citizens living there.

When we left Rome, Ross Elliot was distraught because it meant leaving his dog Tita in Italy. When we boarded the transport to Cairo, I was checking the guys off as they boarded the ship. When Ross came aboard, I noticed that one of his barracks bags was moving. Later I went to him and said, "You've smuggled Tita on board, haven't you?" He said, "Yes, but don't tell anybody." How he managed to train that dog to be quiet and never surface until everyone was asleep, I'll never know. But the dog responded perfectly to the command "Hide."

In Cairo, we did one performance for King Farouk. We didn't realize it but we had been sent there on a diplomatic mission. We were emissaries of good faith. Whatever we were supposed to do, we accomplished. From there, we went to Iran. I flew ahead of the company to Iran to make arrangements for our outfit when we arrived to see whether we should do the larger or smaller version of the show and to make sure they had proper facilities or areas where we could do our show. When I got off the plane in Diszfil, it was 140 degrees and I literally could not breathe. Someone had to pound my chest. The people there live underground in caves, it is so hot. Our guys arrived and there were American troops stationed in other cities in Iran. We did our short version of the show for them. It did so much for these soldiers who had not had a taste of the States until we had arrived.

From Iran, we went to Bombay, India, where we only stayed long enough to board a ship to take us to Australia. We landed in Sydney. Hayden Rorke, one of the members of our company, had a newspaper clipping from home which said that every American GI was to have turkey that Thanksgiving overseas. When we got to Australia, it was Thanksgiving. We had never had turkey, because we moved about so much that all we were ever issued were the Army culinary delicacy called "C-rations." Hayden went to headquarters and raised hell. They finally did give us turkey, but unfortunately it was tainted. There weren't enough latrines to service our company. We were happy to return to our diet of C-rations.

From Australia, we were taken to the Philippines. We did a good little show there for the Philippine government, including a new number I had to do in less than half an hour for Filipino children, who sang a new Irving Berlin song called *Heaven Watch the Philippines*. From the Philippines, we boarded another ship for New Guinea. Ross Elliot had Tita out of his barracks bag, thinking it would be no problem because it was a smaller ship. The officer said Ross couldn't bring Tita on the ship.

We all threatened mutiny. I told the officer, "The dog is a very important part of our show. In the finale, he runs up on stage and carries an American flag in his teeth as the boys are singing our last song." We got Tita on board.

In New Guinea, we entertained mostly Australian soldiers. At Milne Bay in New Guinea, we were finally given our own little ship. It was a small Dutch ship named El Libertador. It was badly in need of repair and a paint job. It was pretty rickety but it was our own and we loved it. Tita loved the ship, too, as he was able to roam about, not confined to quarters. We were on our way to one of the islands and I was standing next to the Dutch captain one night, looking out at the sea, when suddenly a periscope appeared from the water. My heart stopped beating. I whispered to the Captain, "Friendly, no?" He said "No." But he reassured me and said, "Don't worry. They won't do anything. They just see a little Dutch freighter. A small ship. They won't fire at us. Because if they did, we would break security and a plane will be here in less than ten minutes and the sub will be destroyed." The Dutch captain was right. But the sub did follow us for two days. The only person I confided in was Alan Anderson, because he was the First Sergeant, and the Captain had asked me not to discuss it with everyone.

The little ship, slow as it was, got us where we had to be. We traveled to little islands that Bob Hope never heard of and where people had never seen Bob Hope. We played our show for servicemen who had been away from anything that remotely resembled entertainment. They were very appreciative. I don't want to go into too much detail about *This Is The Army*, because Alan Anderson has written a book called *The Last War Song*. It's a very interesting, comprehensive account of *This Is The Army* from it's very inception and I don't want to detract from his account. So, therefore, if some of my stories or approaches seem very cursory, it is done intentionally in deference to Alan Anderson's wonderful book, which you should read.

Our little ship, the El Libertador, fragile as it seemed, rode through a typhoon. It happened one night when we were at sea going to another destination. I was playing cards with Dick Irving, who later in civilian life became a big officer at Universal Studios. We were playing gin rummy and for the first time I was winning. In fact, he was into me for so much of my scrip money – the money the Army issued for its troops overseas – he said, "There's a storm brewing and we better..." I said, "No, no. You sit down." He said, "It's a rough storm." I said, "I don't care how rough it gets, I'm winning. Sit down, we're going to play."

Actually I did get up because although our little ship didn't seem to be in danger, as we looked out onto the horizon, we could see other ships turn over. Literally. Then we saw a raft with men on it. As it got closer to our ship we threw lines down to the men, but unfortunately a big wave engulfed them and we never saw them again.

After this tragedy, we had greater respect for our little El Libertador. Even though it wasn't the cleanest vessel on the ocean, it was certainly the safest. One afternoon at sea, someone inadvertently threw a cigarette, which landed on a tarp that covered the aft part of the ship, and started a fire. Gene Nelson, who later became the dancing star at Warner Brothers Studios, happened to be sunning himself. He sprang into action immediately. We don't know how he did it, but he got the tarp in one hand, ripped it across the ship and dived into the ocean with the flaming tarp in his hand. He really saved our lives, even though he could have killed himself. But Gene was like that. We used to call him the All-American Boy Scout.

We arrived in Manus and played our big show there for some 15,000 seabees, sailors, soldiers and anyone on the island, including some Japanese who were still infiltrating and sniping at people occasionally. In any event, when we got to the island of Manus, we rigged our gear, our platforms and our lights. We had our own generator and we did the show at night. It was going great, until we heard a loudspeaker announce "Air Raid. Air Raid." All of the lights on the island went off except ours, because of our private generator. And they yelled, "Shut that damn thing off." We did. In the dark, I crawled to the edge of the stage and asked our conductor, Milt Rosenstock, who later became Ethel Merman's favorite conductor on Broadway, "Where will we pick it up from when the lights go back on again?" He said, "Letter G." I said, "I don't understand what that means. Hum the part." I went back and told the dancers of that particular number where we were going to pick up the number when the lights came on. I hummed it to them and then sure enough, our generator went on again and the lights came on, as if there had been no interruption of any kind. With perfect coordination, the number continued. These servicemen came crawling back from where

13

they had hidden from what they thought was an air raid. And they were amazed at the spectacle they saw on stage. They cheered. They thought we were heroes. Quite truthfully, it was just another day's work for us.

We then sailed to the Admiralty Islands and did the same large show there. When the show was on, there were Japanese snipers around. As long as there was a musical number going on, they seemed to enjoy that and were quiet. But the minute dialog started, they were annoyed because that didn't please them. And so then two of our comedians, Hank Henry and Jules Oshin, who were well known on Burlesque, were doing a sketch together about our Master Sergeant's mother-in-law with a tattoo on her arm. When the sketch started and they were getting their laughs, the snipers in the trees started shooting at them. They rushed off stage and shouted, "The goddamn enemy is out there shooting at us." I said, "That's not the enemy. Those are critics." Actually, the people on patrol of the island did get rid of the snipers.

We had problems with our advance officers who couldn't do their jobs correctly. They would go to an island and find out where the officers' club was to accommodate their needs, although we couldn't avail ourselves of the benefits of the officers' club. They did not look after our needs – a place to stay and food to eat. After all, we were the ones doing the work. So I would go on ahead to different islands. I remember once going to a PT outfit, which I think they called "Mog Mog." In any event, there was a very nice young commanding officer there named Captain Greene. He didn't pull rank. He knew I was an enlisted man and that we were bringing him the short version of our show. They were grateful for any form of entertainment.

In his tent, which had a wooden floor, there was one officer they all complained about because he was never around. He was always out entertaining the visiting nurses or USO performers because of his father's importance in politics. The young officer was John F. Kennedy. Actually, they were going to put me up for the night in his cot and then Captain Greene thought he should stay there in case he did show up. He might not like to see a stranger in his cot. I never got to see John Kennedy there. But just as with Ronald Reagan, two of our future Presidents crossed our paths.

Captain Greene took me out on a PT boat, an early version of the hydrofoil. I had never been on one. They travel very fast as they skim over the water. We went in and out of little inlets and as we did, sure enough, the snipers were on that island too. They kept firing at us, but Greene laughed because he knew how to dodge those bullets and we got back safely.

I went ahead on one island, and when I arrived, the commanding officer, who mistook me for a USO performer, eventually found out that I was with *This Is The Army*. He said, "I understand you have black boys in your outfit." I said, "Yes, we do. Fourteen of our members are black." He said, "In that case, they'll have to stay in the black camp and the rest of you will stay with us in the white camp." I informed him that we couldn't break up because our orders from General Marshall in Washington definitely stated that we were a unit. We had to stay together and could not be separated. He said, "Very well. In that case, you'll all stay in the black camp." That didn't bother our boys one bit, because we ended up staying together at the black Red Cross in England and it didn't rub off. I was very unhappy, because I suddenly realized that the This Is The Army company was the only integrated company in the history of the American Army. The middle of the Twentieth Century and we were the first integrated outfit. It seemed strange. I couldn't equate that with the land of the free and the home of the brave. That was something that stayed with me throughout the rest of our time in the Army. And it still does.

We went to the Marianas and picked up a ship called the Haleakala, a ship from Hawaii. Compared to the El Libertador, it was like staying in a four-star hotel. We even had our own cabins. The Haleakala took us to Tinian, the island where our B-25 bombers were stationed. That night on our way to the show, we were detained by MPs, who said we had to give right of way because the bombers were on a mission. It was an awesome sight. In two-minute intervals, bombers took off to complete a bombing run. You stood there numb; watching these winged metal arsenals of destruction on their way. You felt how inadequate and useless man could be. Several days after that bombing mission, we heard that the atomic bomb had been dropped on Hiroshima. Although we knew that meant the war was over, we didn't celebrate. A strange pallor had come over us. We had heard the fallout could be very dangerous and could even reach the sea. It could envelope us. It could even reach the States. Of course, we were wrong in our estimate of the danger the bomb could cause. But it definitely marked the end of the war and we were on our way to Hawaii. In Hawaii we drank all the milk we could find. Tita and we were flown back to the States where we were mustered out of the Army.

And so ended the *This Is The Army* odyssey for me. My three and a half years there were the happiest and most enlightening part of my life. *This Is The Army* was our own little utopia. We never had a problem with race, creed or color. Small wonder, we were away from civilization. At a *This Is The Army* reunion, the men were invited to bring their wives along too. And one of the wives complained to me, bitterly. She said, "Do you realize that a night doesn't go by before we go to bed when I have to listen to a *This Is The Army* story from him?" And I said, "How lucky you are, lady. That is the way it should be. To even be associated with *This Is The Army* is an honor and privilege that very few Americans can enjoy." And I was so privileged to be one of those few.

After the War was over and I was out of the Army, I was faced with the reality of being a civilian once more. No longer would Uncle Sam choose and buy my wardrobe, nor would I be subjected to C-rations. Prior to the War, my experience in the working world was only in the theater. I was an assistant choreographer on Broadway and also was a dancer and played small parts. Fortunately, the reality of facing tomorrow wasn't too serious in my case because of my work in the film *This Is The Army*. Several studios were bidding for my services. I finally ended up at Columbia Studios.

From there, I traveled to Broadway, then back to Hollywood. I shuttled back and forth; and in between, I found time to do specials, extravaganzas, expositions and nightclub acts. I was kept pretty busy. Because of all this activity, I got to work with and know some of my show business heroes, whom I have written about and would like you to meet.

Legendary Ladies

Judy Garland

The first time I saw and heard Judy Garland in a film, her magic overpowered and possessed me. It still does and I'm sure it always will. And so, when I was asked to stage the musical numbers for the film version of *Valley of the Dolls*, starring Judy Garland, I jumped at the offer. At last I would get to meet my idol and, more importantly, I would get to work with her. In *Valley of the Dolls*, Andre Prévin wrote the score and there was one song in particular that was perfect for Judy. It had all the drama, the power and the surge that Judy did so well. It was called *I'll Plant My Own Tree*.

With the assistance of my rehearsal pianist, Geoff Clarkson, who actually was the pianist with the Les Brown Orchestra, we worked out an arrangement that we felt would be ideal for her. Judy arrived and she was accompanied by Roger Edens. Roger Edens was probably one of the foremost vocal arrangers in Hollywood. He did all of Judy's work. We played the song for her and I read the lyrics as Geoff played. She stopped us and said, "No, please sing it. I can hear it better that way." I said, "But I don't sing," but she insisted. I said, "My voice would put a foghorn out of business." She said, "Please," and I couldn't resist her, so I started to sing. And I sang right to her, to her eyes, to her face, that wonderful little face. I got carried away. I was acting the thing, I suppose, because when it was over with she said, "It's great! I love it! I love it!" I looked at Roger Edens for a comment and he very haughtily said, "It's quite apparent from your arrangement that you've been listening to all of my work and you've been influenced haven't you?" And I said, "Of course, of course I studied everything you ever did for Judy," which was not the case, but I thought that would win him over and it did.

The very first day of rehearsal, Judy requested that we work in her dressing room when I got there. It was one of the very grand ones right next to the commissary at Twentieth Century Fox, one that's always reserved for superstars. When I got there, I was surprised to see a pool table in the center of the room. I'd heard she'd requested it but I didn't know for what reason. In any case, we started to go over the lyric without a pianist, just walking through business. Well she started to walk all over the place. She was sitting on a table. I sat on a table. She jumped up, she went to a chair – I did that. And finally, she crawled under the pool table. I followed her and I thought that was very odd behavior for anyone, let alone Judy. But then I thought, perhaps that was part of her persona. I didn't question it any further.

However, when we got to the recording stage and she had learned the songs and started to record, Lionel Newman, who was the head of the music department at Fox and conducted the picture, looked at me quizzically as if asking, "What has happened to our girl?" Because it didn't sound anything like Judy Garland. In fact it was very ordinary. I thought, perhaps they were going to do it again at some later date when they said the session was over. I urged Lionel to get hold of the waxed playback copy, the one you use on the stage, because I knew if someone got hold of that they could bootleg it and issue recordings of Judy Garland's voice at it's worst. We managed to get that out of the hands of anyone that had that in mind.

The very first day of shooting, Judy arrived very early as scheduled. She went to make-up, had her hair and wardrobe done, and was on the set by 8:30 am. At 9:00 am when she was called to the stage she refused to open her dressing room door. Fox had heard rumors about her behavior and they had security there to make sure there was no liquor or, possibly, drugs around, but she still would not open her dressing room door to anyone. Finally, time passed, it got later and later and the head of Fox called the shoot off and dismissed everyone. I didn't leave; I thought it was my duty to be there when my star made her entrance. After six, she did make her entrance, a very studied entrance. She came on the stage expecting the adulation of her former friends, when she suddenly realized nobody was there. And in a very plaintive voice she cried, "Where is everyone? Where is everyone?" I said, "They've gone home." And Judy said, "How could they leave me? Why would they leave me?" and she sat down and cried. Sadly, I realized this was the end of Judy's career. But yet I believe her magic will never disappear. It will always be out there somewhere waiting for new audiences to discover old Judy Garland films and become possessed and overpowered by her talent, as I was the first time I saw her.

Lucille Ball

Two of my army buddies - Hayden Rorke, who played Captain Bellows in the TV series *I Dream of Jeannie,* and Jus Addiss, who was an assistant director in films - produced a revival of a comedy called *Dream Girl.* The central character in *Dream Girl* could be a showcase, a *tour de force,* if played by the right performer. Hayden and Jus were convinced they did have the right performer in their dear friend Lucy.

A former Goldwyn showgirl, she had been around a bit, yet she was taken for granted and nothing happened for her until opening night, when a new star was born: Miss Lucille Ball. It was the most incredible performance I'd ever witnessed. She practically climbed walls; she did every trick burlesque comediennes never thought of. It became a triumph for her. It really brought her to the attention of the town.

Fortunately for Lucy, the Broadway and Hollywood stars refused to work in the new medium of television (it was beneath them) and consequently TV producers had no choice but to use new talent. Lucy Ball was ideal for them because they had just seen her performance in *Dream Girl.* So they produced a pilot for their new star but unfortunately it was a failure, a dismal flop. Any other young actress would have taken to the hills to hibernate, but not Lucille Ball. She was determined to prove that she was not a failure and she hocked everything she owned. She mortgaged her house and raised enough money to do another pilot, only this time there would be a change in production. It was all to be done her way and her way proved to be the right way. Her way gave us *I Love Lucy* and no one can argue with that.

Throughout Lucille's career, her "we'll do it my way" format brought her the fame and recognition she deserved. I directed a Tennessee Ernie Ford special. The guest stars were Lucille Ball and Andy Griffith, a deft comedian whose characterization of a country boy made *No Time for Sergeant* and *The Andy Griffith Show* the successes they were.

In the special, there was a scene for Lucy and Andy. It was a pantomime of a young couple living in a trailer. Lucy couldn't be there at the beginning of rehearsals and she asked me to lay out her sketch and play the part, which I did. The trailer was so small, one person could barely fit into it comfortably, so two people would be out of the question. I quickly realized that's where the comedy was: two people living in that crowded condition. So Andy and I invented little "bits and pieces" that had to do with going about your daily business but not being able to move very easily. Consequently, there were times when Andy would get it in the eye because Lucy was reaching for a pan. Or when Andy was up trying to get a light on and Lucy was below trying to reach for eggs to make breakfast, he'd lower his arm and he'd practically strangle her. It all was hoke, but it was good hoke and it was the sort of thing we knew Lucy would like and we did work the thing out rather well, I thought. I enjoyed playing the part so much that I hoped Lucy would never show up, but she did.

We ran the sketch for her and I could tell by the expression on her face that she really liked it; she couldn't wait to dive in and take over. She said, "This piece of business is good but we should change it this way," and "This would be better if you stretched it a little more," or "You should eliminate this." And Andy and I both smiled because we knew we had come up with a good sketch and we also knew that Lucy had to do it her way. How could you argue with her, when that very week it was announced that Lucille Ball and Company had bought RKO studios? It was a great honor for Lucy to be the first female to own a major studio. Not bad for a former showgirl who did it her way.

Lena Horne

Lena Horne had a way with a song. She could be tantalizing, inviting, daring, challenging, lustful or just plain sexy. If Lena ever recorded *The Lord's Prayer*, she could convert more non-believers than any hellfire, brimstone preacher man ever did. I first met Lena backstage at the Capitol Theater in New York City where she was appearing. I was there visiting a dance act called "The Dunhills," who were friends of mine, and they introduced me to Lena. That afternoon she was very upset. Lena had reason to be upset. Apparently, the weekly magazine *Ebony* wrote a scathing article about her. They accused her of not mingling with her own people and trying to cross over to the whites. This article finally ended up calling her an "Uncle Tom", which was not very flattering.

I next saw Lena in Paris where she was to appear at the Baccarat Nightclub on the Champs-Elysées. She arrived some ten days before her opening because she wanted to adjust to her new environment and to get the feel of the French people. A very close friend of mine, Jimmy Gardiner, a Texas oilman and Broadway producer, knew Lena quite well. So the three of us sort of did the town, showing Lena the sights. We would spend a lot of time discussing her opening, because she was very apprehensive, she was really frightened about it. She thought maybe they wouldn't like her. Jimmy had a good idea. He said, "You know Lena, if you're wise, you'll have one of the couturiers design a thing for you to wear opening night. I can arrange it for you; I can get them to do it. I know you have your own wardrobe, but wear something special, something like a boa or a cape." And Lena was very grateful and decided she would do just that.

Opening night for Lena at the Baccarat was a triumph. Not since Josephine Baker had anyone made such an impression on the French public. She was the talk of Paris. Yet she was happy when her engagement ended, even though she knew she could remain in Paris and work everywhere, probably live there just like Josephine Baker did. But not Lena, she wanted to come back to the States where she belonged, especially Las Vegas and the Sands Hotel where she was the reigning queen. Jack Entratta, the entertainment director at the Sands Hotel, chose Lena above everyone else as his favorite performer. That was a big order because the Rat Pack – Frank Sinatra, Sammy Davis, Jr., Dean Martin and company – all played there. But in Jack's book Lena was number one.

I remember one New Year's night when Lena was playing the Sands. She was going to give a party after the show and I was invited of course. In the audience was one of her greatest fans, one of her biggest fans, Clint Eastwood. Clint knew that I knew Lena and he asked if he could meet her. I asked Lena if I could bring him backstage. She said, "No. Bring him to the party." When I told Clint he was invited to the party his face broke out into the biggest smile in place of the usual scowl he wore. He behaved like an adolescent. It really made his evening.

Lena broke all social tradition at the Sands. She was probably the first black performer ever permitted to actually stay, sleep and live at the same hotel where she worked. At that time, most black performers, even headliners, could play the big hotels but they couldn't live there. One day at the Sands, this bigoted woman came flying into the office and wanted to see the manager. Jack Entratta happened to be there. He said, "What's the problem madam?" And she said, "There's a black person in the swimming pool." The black person was Lena's daughter, Gail. Jack said, "And?" She said, "I want her out of that pool or I check out." Jack said, "Ma'am, may I carry your bags now?"

Lena had strange fixations about herself. She hated to listen to her recordings and she really thought that she was ugly. This great exotic beauty truly believed that. Lena performed a one-woman show in every major city in the United States. As in Paris, she was triumphant. Her loyal audiences were there cheering her on.

The magic of Lena had to be seen. It was never captured on a recording or on film. But when you were in the audience watching her, your emotions were raised to the highest level you had ever known. This woman was magic. At the height of her career, she gave up performing and retired. No one seems to know why and many of her dear friends don't hear from her anymore. So all we have left of Lena is a memory that only people who saw her perform can appreciate.

Betty Grable

Betty Grable was as much at home rolling dice in a gambling casino as she was in a rehearsal hall going over one of her dance routines. She and her husband, the famous bandleader Harry James, were inveterate gamblers. They would bet on anything. In fact, they lost a small fortune on a 660-acre tract of land they had near North Hollywood, where they raised horses. Unfortunately, they couldn't pay their income tax so the government stepped in and took it from them. It didn't cure Betty one bit. Every season at the racetrack in Del Mar, she had her box, and would even rent a house so she could live close to the races. Later, she moved to Las Vegas where she and Harry had a house near the casinos that they loved so well.

One time I was in Vegas and Betty and I were going to see the nightclub act of some performer we knew. As we were walking through the casino, I said, "I feel lucky." She said, "Really?" I said, "Yes, I do." She turned to one of the croupiers and she said, "Let me have five and put it on seven on the come out." And sure enough she lost and I was very embarrassed. I said, "Betty, I think I should pay you the five dollars." But she said, "No dear, it's more like five hundred. But it doesn't matter." She had credit in any hotel and could ask for any amount she wanted. They knew she was good for it.

I did the first CBS colorcast on television starring Betty Grable. We had a lot of laughs during rehearsal. Betty would feign being ill because she hated to rehearse; she only wanted to perform. One day during rehearsals, some of the big wigs from CBS came to visit and they were there to have some pictures taken with Betty for a publicity release. Betty told them, "Just a few please because I must rush home, someone at my house is ill." They were genuinely disturbed and they said, "Betty, you should have gone home earlier." She said, "No, I had a job to do you know. The show must go on." And she took off. Actually, she was rushing home to get the latest racetrack results on one particular program that came on at a certain hour.

In spite of her image as the original pin-up girl with the most beautiful legs in the world, Betty felt more comfortable covering those legs with a pair of slacks. She was not one of the Beverly Hills crowd. She was not one of the Hollywood crowd. She never behaved like a star. Betty was more comfortable with some of her Polish friends than she was with some of the movie celebrities. Incidentally, she was really quite popular with so many stars who tried hard to become her friend. She was very polite but that never did happen. One persistent Hollywood personality was Joan Crawford, who was determined to make Betty her friend. She would always call Betty to invite her to different functions, but Betty would always have some excuse.

This one particular day, Joan phoned Betty and said, "I have some friends coming from England, they're wonderful people and you must meet them." Betty said, "I'd love to but unfortunately the maids didn't show up today and I have to scrub these floors, they're filthy." Betty said the wrong thing because Joan Crawford, who was called "Miss Tidy", loved nothing more than scrubbing walls and scrubbing floors. She told Betty that she'd be right over. Well, poor Betty had to change into something that's suitable for scrubbing floors. Joan Crawford did arrive and so the two of them spent the afternoon cleaning Betty's house.

Once, after a rehearsal, Betty had possibly had one drink too many. She wasn't drunk, a little tipsy perhaps. While she was on her way home, the light changed. The woman in front of her stopped her car abruptly and Betty's bumper tapped the lady's car. The woman got out and raised all sorts of hell. She was screaming, "You ruined my car," although she really hadn't. So they exchanged licenses. Betty's license always read "Mrs. Betty James"; after all, she was Mrs. James. The woman wrote the name down and then suddenly looked up and said, "Aren't you Betty Grable?" And Betty snapped at her and said, "How dare you mistake me for that slut?"

A Betty Grable film was always among the top box office grosses in the industry. Her studio, Twentieth Century Fox, benefited greatly from Betty's work – more than once she bailed them out of a difficult financial situation. In fact, in one instance, she actually saved the studio from bankruptcy. Betty never made waves; she could have held the studio up for more money but she didn't. She was a true star, one of the most easy to get along with. When Betty died, sadly there weren't too many people at the church. The only celebrities present were Jackie

Robert Sidney

Coogan, her first husband, Harry James, her last husband, Alice Faye, Mitzi Gaynor, Cesar Romero and Dan Dailey. Of course, all the chorus people she had worked with were there, as were the wardrobe women, the stagehands and the technicians. The people Betty really loved. As for the Beverly Hills and the Hollywood crowd, they were a "no-show", as one says at the racetrack. Betty would have laid you odds on that and she would have won.

Alice Faye

Nick Vanoff, the producer of the variety show *The Hollywood Palace* phoned me and said, "I want you to do a number for Alice Faye, who has agreed to come out of her retirement and appear on the show." I was very flattered to be considered so highly by Nick. So there I was working out a number with the boys that would support Alice. I made sure I chose older dancers because they would complement Alice and would provide a good background for her. However, Nick failed to tell me that Alice agreed to appear on his show only if she could pre-record the song and lip-sync to it, and be photographed in close-ups. She did not want to do any number of any kind.

When the boys and I were rehearsing, Alice arrived. When I saw her I melted. I immediately thought of the film *Hello Frisco, Hello*, in which she sang *You'll Never Know*. No matter how long you're in this business, when you're in the company of a legend something happens. It's so exhilarating. You can't even describe it. Alice explained she had come by to tell us why she couldn't possibly do the number: she'd be scared stiff. She hoped we'd understand and she also hoped that the boys wouldn't lose their jobs. As she was talking, I took her arm and I started walking with her and I'm sure she thought I wanted to get her away from the boys so we could have a private conversation. She was going on about how insecure she was, as she hadn't been near a camera or a stage in so long. I said, "Alice, do you realize that you needn't be afraid, because you've done half the number now." She said, "I don't know what you mean." I said, "As we were walking around, I moved you in different positions and we turned once or twice, and those are the first sixteen bars of the number you're going to do." She said, "Oh you dog!"

On the night of her performance, the thunderous applause should have assured Alice that she need not be concerned about appearing in front of an audience. Their love for her was so enthusiastic and so outgoing. They were thrilled to have Alice back where she belonged – on a stage.

When Alice was to appear on *The Dean Martin Show*, she phoned me and said, "I hope you're putting together a good energetic dance number, because I really want to do one." It was a completely different Alice. She arrived and we did do energetic dance things for her. She loved every moment of it. She had complete confidence in herself. She had no hang-ups about being afraid of an audience or being insecure. In fact, on the last show she did, she insisted upon ending the number we did for her with a lift. The boys threw her up in the air and caught her. It could be dangerous, but she insisted upon doing it.

When Alice decided to return to show business, it wasn't because she needed the money. On the contrary, Alice's brother invested her money very wisely when she was a big star at Twentieth Century Fox. He bought her some land on Wilshire Boulevard in Beverly Hills. And anyone who has land on Wilshire Boulevard in Beverly Hills need never worry about rainy days or the future. Alice returned to show business because she genuinely loved being among its people. She felt comfortable with "show people" because she spoke their language. Any insecurity she might have would dissipate when she sat down with some of her buddies from the good old days. Alice will always remain a legendary star in books on the movie industry and also in the memory of those of us who saw her or knew her and loved her.

Legendary
Gentlemen

Dick Powell

After hanging around for weeks waiting for production to start on *Susan Slept Here*, starring Dick Powell and Debbie Reynolds, I was finally called to the office of its producer Harriet Parsons. Harriet was the daughter of the renowned columnist Louella Parsons, who was so powerful she could make you or break you in her column if she chose. It would be less regrettable to offend the Pope than to offend Louella. At the meeting were Frank Tashlin, the writer/director, and one of its two stars, Dick Powell. I kept staring at Dick Powell and thinking of those good old Warner Brothers musicals he starred in, musicals that made me want to be part of the business. I could almost hear him singing *Lullaby of Broadway*, *I've Gotta Sing A Torch Song* and *42nd Street*. I was so busy lost in my memory that I didn't hear him tell me that he didn't dance.

When the meeting was over with and we said goodbye, Dick Powell said "I'm afraid you didn't hear me, I said I don't dance." I said, "No, not you too! This seems to be a chronic condition with this company. You can't dance, Anne Francis is no threat to Cyd Charisse, and Alvey Moore can hardly walk, let alone dance. Fortunately, Debbie Reynolds can dance, that will help. Incidentally, can you do a waltz?" He said, "You mean the kind of waltz you do in social dancing?" I said, "Exactly." He said, "Oh I can do that." I said, "Fine, if you can do a waltz I can do the rest. I'll make you look so good that when people see you on the screen, they will think you are a dancer. Of course, you never will be." And that was the end of our visit.

The script of *Susan Slept Here* indicated there was to be a ballet done by the four principals. Of course, they never indicated what this ballet was about nor did they suggest the concept of the ballet. It was left up to me, I suppose. I felt this was a challenge. If I could make it work, it would be the first time in the business a number was done with non-dancers (except for Debbie) without using "dance-ins" as doubles. It also might advance the plot and cut out pages of dialogue. I started working with Debbie Reynolds, since she was the only one who could dance. I thought whatever we designed in terms of the ballet would revolve around her. My assistant Ellen Ray gave Debbie *ballet barre* every morning to warm her up before we started working on combinations.

One day, Dick Powell appeared and said, "What are you guys up to?" I said, "We're doing a *ballet barre* to warm up." He asked if he could join. I said, "Of course." I was amused and amazed that he actually got in there and tried to do all the stretches that one does in ballet. I admired his courage and after that he did come in more often. He and Debbie got to know each other well. One day I said to Dick, "Why don't you do a waltz with Debbie?" And he said, "Come on Debbie, let's do it!" She said, "You know I don't know how to waltz." And I thought, "Oh no, this will never happen." Finally they did waltz and curiously enough just doing that waltz together – the movement, two people dancing close to each other – got them closer together than the script ever did.

The ballet I created for Debbie was a dream sequence where she thinks she's a canary bird in a cage that Dick Powell is carrying, when he is distracted by a siren, namely Anne Francis, who beckons to him. He drops the cage and goes to Anne; Debbie desperately tries to get out of the cage and finally does so in time to find Dick about to marry Anne Francis. She interrupts the ceremony, fighting all the way to the finish to get rid of Anne Francis, which she does. But just as she thinks she's triumphant with Dick, she awakens and realizes it is a dream and sobs into her pillow. It was a charming sequence and became an important part of the picture.

The picture, incidentally, was a great success and the reviewers were very, very kind to Dick. They were happy to see him back in a musical film. One of the reviewers said they didn't know that Dick Powell was a good dancer. When I read the review I said to Dick, "Well you could fool me." In any case, Dick and I became good friends. I would go to visit him in his house in Mandeville Canyon and reunited with June Allyson, whom I had known in New York. We were a happy trio. One day Dick asked me whether I would like to work on a picture with June Allyson and a newcomer Jack Lemmon. The picture was called *You Can't Run Away From It.* It was a musical remake of *It Happened One Night,* which starred Clark Gable and Claudette Colbert.

Working with Dick brought us very close together. I got to know him quite well. I noticed that even when he was unhappy or disturbed or upset he would always whistle or hum or sing one of the songs he knew. I could tell by the way he sang or hummed what his particular mood

31

was. And I was there to help him solve any immediate problems that he might have – we were really that close.

After *You Can't Run Away From It*, he called me. There was a long dance sequence in a film he was directing called *The Conqueror*, starring John Wayne and Susan Hayward. Here again the sequence has a story point in the script and I thought, "Will I ever get to do an out-and-out dance routine with real dancers and without any story lines or advancing of the plot?" But Dick had called me, so I was there. Actually, it was a very interesting sequence because it involved different kinds of tribal dancing that ended with Susan Hayward, who does her dance only because it's a ploy to get a dagger and try to kill John Wayne.

When we started to shoot the sequence, Dick was very upset and finally admitted to me, "I waited until the last minute and probably should have told you earlier, but Howard Hughes and his cronies insist that we use this particular group of girl dancers who are here on the set now." I told him, "Those girls did audition for me. I think the only time they're on their feet and not on their backs is when they auditioned this afternoon. They can't dance! They're much better off in a prone position."

But then I thought, "Why not?" I said, "Dick, I have a crazy idea. Let's get some divans and some pillows and drape the pillows around the girls and have the camera actually embrace each girl, investigate each girl, almost seduce each girl so it's as if the camera's having sex with each girl. It will please Howard Hughes and his henchmen and it might be deliciously vulgar." We did just that. From there we panned over to the dance sequence. The whole thing is quite stylish, in spite of the gals on the sofa. That part is quite interesting from a pornographic point of view. But I did my job with Dick and once more our friendship was stronger than ever.

In *The Conqueror*, Dick was on location in St. George, Utah and there was a rumor going around that all members of *The Conqueror* company were exposed to fallout from atomic bomb experiments the U.S. government was conducting. It was believed that Dick developed cancer as a result. From *The Conqueror* he went on to start his Four Star Company, which was very successful in producing television shows. He invited me to join him in an executive position. But before I did, Dick's cancer unfortunately got worse and he finally left us.

I was devastated by Dick Powell's death, not because he gave me work, but because he gave me his friendship. He was a dear, important friend to me. We had a strong kind of friendship that one rarely gets in life. He was concerned, he was warm, he shared your problems, and he was there when I needed advice. He meant so much to me that when he died he took a part of me with him. It's not easy to mourn someone you cared about so much.

Jack Lemmon

The first time I saw Jack Lemmon, all I could think of was Ivy League and a cast member of one of the *Hasty Pudding* shows at Harvard. There was nothing about him that suggested the theatre or movies. He was a rather wholesome-looking man. He might have been a car salesman or a young lawyer, but certainly not an actor. I was just as surprised as other people were when Dick Powell announced that he had chosen Jack Lemmon to play opposite June Allyson in the musical remake of *It Happened One Night*. It was called *You Can't Run Away From It*. I knew Dick must have had a reason to choose Jack Lemmon over all the available leading men who had great track records. But Dick was firm, he would not have anyone else play the part but Jack Lemmon. I couldn't understand why.

The first day I came on the set when they were shooting a scene. I thought this Jack Lemmon was pretty flip. He was talking to people instead of waiting for someone to say "action" or "roll 'em." But he wasn't talking to anybody, he was acting – he was so natural. I thought this man has a special quality, with his nuances and subtle takes. He fascinated me because the last time I saw someone act like that on film was good old Spencer Tracey. I realized then why Dick Powell chose him to play opposite June Allyson.

In the original *It Happened One Night*, Claudette Colbert plays a runaway heiress and Clark Gable is a newspaper man who recognizes her. In one particular scene, they are obliged to spend the night in a motel and in order to get the room they have to register as husband and wife. Because of Clark Gable's sensual and Claudette Colbert's physical qualities, it wasn't conceivable to me that these two people shared a hotel room together without consummating their so-called "marriage." Whereas, when Jack Lemmon and June Allyson do the very same scene, which is done as a musical number, you accept them sharing a twin bed and room together. Because they're both so wholesome and clean, you can easily conceive that they could very well spend a night together and still be at odds.

Jack on location was somewhat special. If there was a little upright piano around he would run over and play his music and sing. He was our source of entertainment on the road. There was a special scene we did in Tucson where Jack and June are trying to hitch a ride and he tries everything he knows and it doesn't work. June, as in the original, just steps up and says, "Watch this!" And it's done as a musical number. She lifts her skirt and this horrible broken car does stop, backing up to give them a lift. Jack and June get in the car. Jack's in the back of this Jeep sitting on the edge with the suitcases as they're yelling, "roll 'em" and the Jeep took off. But it took off with a start and a jolt and Jack landed right on his head. Naturally, they yelled, "Cut!" Jack said, "Oh no, why didn't you get that? That was wonderful! Let's try it again!" He was willing to get up on this thing and fall deliberately on his head. Of course, Dick Powell knew that the company insurance wouldn't allow that. But Jack was very cooperative. He was very keen. What I liked best about his performance is that his line readings were so unconventional and yet so brilliantly natural.

We also had a location spot at the Hotel del Coronado in San Diego, which is the most charming, old hotel – very special. We had extras on location and Jack had quite a lot to do in this particular scene on the next morning's shoot. But the night before, one of our extras who thought he had to sort of, I guess you'd say "fix Jack up" with a girl, got Jack to drink a few drinks and then some more drinks. Obviously, Jack was not the drinking type. Our room was right next door and I knew he was in trouble because he was almost retching and this guy persistently said, "Now this girl . . ." I just barged in and said, "Hey, out! If you want to be on this location, if you want your job, you get out right now!" I got a hold of Jack, who really was sick. I got him in a cold shower and he still was heaving. Poor Jack, the next morning I thought, he'll never make the call. He was there bright and early reading lines as though he had been up all night – not carousing about, but studying his part.

Dick Quine, who directed *How To Murder Your Wife* starring Jack Lemmon and Verna Lisi, a beautiful, blonde Italian girl, was having trouble with a scene that he thought they could shoot without a proper rehearsal. It was a wild party, with everybody celebrating, perhaps with one drink too many. They thought I could stage it for them.

So I got there and took Jack aside as I realized the only way to do it would be from the point of view of Jack's character. I said to Jack, "You know about drinking. You remember the Hotel del Coronado?" He glowered at me and mouthed, "You son-of-a-****!" Then I said, "Just no matter what happens, try to reach Verna Lisi, because apparently she's the one you are in love with." I got hold of a few girls who were extras on the set – one happened to have been a dancer – and I said, "fall on Jack and never let go." Poor Jack was struggling, with all these girls in his way, to reach Verna Lisi and the scene worked beautifully. Dick Quine came to me afterwards and asked, "How could you put that together so quickly?" I replied, "I couldn't have done it without the help of Jack Lemmon, because he's an authority on drunken scenes and he made many wise suggestions that I used, and that's why the scene worked."

I next worked with Jack at the great benefit for the Motion Picture Home for retired people in the film industry honoring Frank Sinatra. I staged the number *Hello, Dolly* for Pearl Bailey. Instead of using regular chorus boys we used Jack Lemmon, Don Rickles, David Niven, Rock Hudson, Sammy Davis, Jr. and Joe Namath. I thought it would be wise to give each one of these very expensive chorus boys a little solo of his own. Jack started the number and I showed him what a traveling time step looked like during our rehearsals for the show. He had his own version of it, which was not meant to be that outrageously funny. But any kind of step by him would be funny because he walked like a penguin and he danced like two of them. The audience was howling. He carried it off beautifully. In fact, he liked what he did so much, he hoped we could do the number at another benefit.

I found Jack to be an incredibly talented actor and the industry only thought of him as a comedian until he finally did a very dramatic role in *Days of Wine and Roses*, a performance for which he was nominated for Academy Award. I believe that Jack could have attained great heights in the theatre if he had ever got to play Hamlet. His nuances and his subtle delivery of lines would have given us a Hamlet that we've never seen or heard before, and it would have been a very interesting one. Of course, now we shall never know whether he could have played Hamlet that well or not. However, if consistency of excellent performances means anything, definitely Jack Lemmon would have made a brilliant Hamlet.

Lionel Newman

Every year in Hollywood around Oscar time, the town is buzzing and speculating on who will be nominated for an Oscar. One of the safest and surest bets is to put your money on a member of the Newman clan. They have dominated Oscar nominations for music awards year after year with few exceptions. It all started with Alfred Newman, the patriarch. Once he won his Oscar it followed that at least one member of the Newman family would be nominated from then on. Lionel Newman, Alfred's younger brother, followed suit. And Randy Newman just won an Oscar in 2002.

When I got to work on *Bloodhounds on Broadway* at Twentieth Century Fox, I met with Lionel Newman, who had been assigned as the musical director of the picture. He and I were at odds immediately. He had asked me to use a rehearsal pianist whom I didn't think qualified for the sort of work I planned to do. I told Lionel I needed another pianist, I didn't like this one. Lionel insisted I use this one and immediately the fight was on between us. I left Lionel and went to his brother Alfred's office to complain. I said, "Look, I cannot use the pianist your brother has assigned to me and I find your brother impossible to work with. He's difficult, he's rude, he's a bully, he's threatening . . ." Alfred interrupted me and said, "Surely Lionel has one good quality." I said, "If you find it, it will be the greatest discovery since King Tut's Tomb." Alfred assured me that there was no problem, things would work out very well and everybody would be satisfied, and he also welcomed me to Twentieth Century Fox Studios.

That afternoon, I was having lunch with my assistant Ellen Ray and I saw Lionel come into the commissary. I said, "Oh no, he's heading to my table." He did, he came right to the table and he announced that it was kind of me to invite him and that he was terribly sorry he was late for lunch. And then he sat down. Of course, I never had invited him. He told Ellen, "I've been so busy spending the morning trying to find the proper pianist for a very temperamental friend of mine." I got up and said, "I've had enough!" He said, "Why don't you sit down, people will think we're having a fight." He got up and kissed me in front of everyone in the commissary. I was absolutely speechless! From that day on, Lionel and I became very close. In fact, Lionel and I were seen so often together people were beginning to wonder.

Lionel was a master of the four-letter word. It wasn't offensive somehow when that big mouth of his uttered these censurable, chosen bits of dialogue. He had his own way of describing people. Mitzi Gaynor was very young at the time and cute and plump. He called her "Bubble Ass." And Betty Grable was "Diamond Lil." He also had several names for me, one more offensive than the other. But that was his way of showing affection. He even had a name for the head of the studio, Darryl Zanuck, whom he called "The Midas Midget."

The picture *Bloodhounds on Broadway* was working on a very limited budget and so we didn't have attractive scenery. I thought we could do this one number just using lights against the black curtain. The technician said there would be a leakage and wouldn't work, but I insisted that we try it. We did and it worked beautifully. That was an innovation of sorts because up to that time I don't think that sort of theatre (Broadway lighting) was ever used in a film. Lionel was very proud, he ran around telling everyone that his friend, meaning me, did a very, very good job. You'd have thought he was my agent the way he touted me. He also had a concern. He said, "I'm afraid my friend is too inventive for this place, they'll probably boot him out of the studio."

I got to know Lionel's family very well, his dear wife Beverly and their three children Carol, Deborah and Jennifer. At home, Lionel was a little more guarded with his expletives, possibly because of the children. Beverly and Lionel made a great team. They were very much in love, maybe because they were complete opposites. Beverly Newman was naïve and sometimes didn't quite understand some of the things Lionel was saying. But it didn't matter because Lionel was saying them and she loved him. I once was on a trip to Las Vegas with Lionel, Beverly and the rest of the Newman clan. We were on one of those B-25s, the plane that had two seats on either side of an aisle. I was sitting next to Lionel and Beverly was sitting opposite me, next to one of her sisters-in-law. The rest of the plane was filled with Lionel's many brothers and their wives. The stewardess came by and she asked Lionel for his name, she was checking her passenger log. He said, "Lionel Newman." She asked me for my name and before I could answer he said, "Mrs. Lionel Newman." Then she looked across Beverly's side and said to Beverly,

"Your name?" And Beverly said, "Mrs. Lionel Newman." She said, "You can't be – he is." We never knew if she was serious or she was putting us on. We had something to talk about for the rest of the trip.

When Alfred Newman retired from Twentieth Century Fox, Lionel succeeded him and it wasn't nepotism. Lionel was a musical genius. Lionel's background was quite astonishing. When he was sixteen, he conducted Earl Carroll's theatre restaurant in Miami. At the age of twenty-one he conducted *Earl Carroll's Vanities,* a very important girly show with all the most beautiful nudes that competed with the *Ziegfield Follies.* It was then that he met his wife Beverly. She was Earl Carroll's niece and Earl Carroll had created an executive assistant job for her so she would have something to do. I think that Lionel was so busy seeing nudes for the early part of his life, that when he met Beverly, who was fully clothed, he fell in love with her.

He finally ended up at Fox, where he stayed for many years. Of course, he too, as Alfred before him, won an Oscar. Actually it was for conducting and scoring *Hello Dolly* with Barbra Streisand. Lionel and I both worked on two Academy Award® shows and we really were outrageous. We'd go to these board meetings filled with very staid, conservative, serious people and Lionel would begin his blasphemy using me as the object of that affection. It got to be that they looked forward to our meetings; however, I always felt that Lionel and I should never be seen in public together.

At Twentieth Century Fox, he encouraged and developed some very talented people. It was Lionel who recognized that a young pianist named John Williams could score brilliantly. And John Williams, as you know, apart from being the conductor of the Boston Pops has also won Oscars for some of the best music for films. Lionel also did the same for Jerry Goldsmith.

Lionel would also call me into the office on some pretext. It usually wasn't anything important; he was just bored and wanted to have some laughs. We both would be outrageous when he had some serious composer there. The poor man couldn't wait to leave the room, we were so embarrassing. Lionel got ill suddenly; it was a chest problem and he was in Cedars Sinai Hospital. He was there two or three days and I tried to get up to see him. But, unfortunately, his doctors decided that he was to have no visitors except immediate family and I never got a chance to say goodbye to him because he left so quickly. Sometimes when I'm angry and I use some of the swear words that I grew up with hanging around Lionel Newman, I almost believe it's Lionel urging me to say those words.

The Choreographers

George Balanchine

George Balanchine, the master of the dance, loved dance as passionately as he loved women. Let's face it, George Balanchine was a womanizer. Not because he was married five times, but because he always managed to have an extramarital affair waiting in the wings, as it were. He didn't have to stray far from home base. Balanchine only fooled around with dancers. His wives, in proper sequence, were: Alexandra Danilova, famed ballerina; Tamara Geva, Broadway musical dancing star; Vera Zorina, another ballerina; Maria Tallchief, a ballerina and exceptional pianist; and his last wife, Tanaquil Le Clerque, who unfortunately become an invalid.

Balanchine was a graduate of the prestigious Maryinsky Theater School for the Arts in Russia. Even though he was interested in dance, he was obliged to study music, painting, history of the arts and draftsmanship. All these other studies paid off very well for Mr. Balanchine, because as a consequence of having studied all those subjects he was a very talented pianist, a good draftsman and, of course, the brilliant choreographer we know. Balanchine rebelled against the staid, conservative, rigid regimen of the ballet. He didn't approve of a ballerina who worried more about the position of her feet when she was dancing than the movement of her body. He believed that the *barre* was the place where you worked on technique and all the rigid laws of ballet. However, once the dancer left the *barre*, he wanted complete freedom in their dancing. He wanted them to totally ignore what they learned at the *barre* and be free. In fact, that freedom is one quality in all of his ballets that appeals to the audience.

In Ballanchine's ballet *Apollon Musegète*, Apollo and the three muses dance wildly, exotically, as they intertwine their bodies and never let go of their hands. It was a masterpiece of construction and George Balanchine at his very best.

Balanchine had a curiosity about other areas of the dance. Broadway fascinated him. He jumped at the chance to choreograph the musical *On Your Toes*. In it, he created a ballet called *Slaughter on Tenth Avenue*. It was very revolutionary for ballet to appear in a Broadway musical at that time. It was a great success and ballets were not that uncommon in musicals from then on. He also did the same for films when he choreographed a ballet for Vera Zorina in the *Goldwyn Follies*. That too was revolutionary and was critically acclaimed.

Balanchine was a gifted craftsman, but unfortunately he couldn't exhibit his art because it would have been censored. He and his friend the modern painter Tchelechiv, had a favorite pastime. They both liked to sit around and make pen and ink sketches, pornographic in nature and Rabelaisian in content, the subject matter always a monk and a nun. No respectable gallery would dare risk an exhibition of their work. Balanchine exhibited his talent as a musician when he was having a problem with the tempos in the musical *Keep Off the Grass*, which he had choreographed. He and the conductor got into a bit of an argument and finally the conductor grabbed him and said, "If I only understood your English perhaps I could help." Balanchine simply answered, "I show," sat down at the piano and played so beautifully it sounded like a full orchestra. From then on there was never a question about tempos again.

Balanchine fancied himself a good cook and his secret formula was good brandy and lots of it. When you had dinner at his house, after the first course you were so tipsy, you thought what he had prepared had been the best meal you had ever tasted. We owe Balanchine so much. He influenced our culture. He inspired young dancers and future choreographers and he gave us, the audience, such pleasure. It will be a long time before the world meets an architectural giant in the dance such as George Balanchine.

Jack Cole

Jack Cole early in his career was a member of the highly respected Denis-Shawn Dance Company. They featured in their repertoire East Indian and Oriental dancing. They were one of the favorites on the concert tour and usually had a sell-out audience. This one day, because of an error on the part of their agent, instead of being booked into a concert hall, they had been booked into a smoke-filled nightclub. Panic set in. The orchestra rehearsal was a disaster. Miss Ruth St. Denis, "Miss Ruth" as she was lovingly called, finally came up with a solution. She stoically asked the bandleader if he had any Eastern music and he said, "Yes, a thing called *In a Persian Market*. She said, "Let's hear it." The only thing Persian about it was the title. However, she got the group together and said, "We will dance to this music but we will count our way. Count our way; remember that. 'One and two and three and four, two and . . .'" and so on.

That night in front of a really loud, half-drunk audience they appeared and for some strange reason the audience was more than receptive. They were fascinated to hear the music and to watch the strange dancing in front of them. The dancers were not flattered by the reception, all they wanted was to leave and forget this horrible experience. Jack Cole, however, did not forget this horrible experience. In fact he remembered it vividly when he staged his first nightclub act for himself and the Kraft Sisters, who excelled in East Indian dancing. Once again the jazz beat behind Indian dancing worked as successfully as it did the night the Denis-Shawn Dance Company appeared in that smoke-filled nightclub.

Jack Cole sensed he was on to something original. At the time, he didn't realize he was laying the foundation for a new dance form. But from then on the jazz beat was the background for all of the music he danced to. He organized a nightclub act for himself and a group of dancers that was highly successful in all the nightclubs they played. Jack Cole was then signed by Columbia Studios in Hollywood. They allowed him to get a skeleton group together, ostensibly to work out numbers for future productions. Jack used his own dance group from his nightclub act and, happily, it was a very good arrangement for him because he knew his dancers and their capabilities. But he worked them almost to exhaustion. He wanted so much from them. He even had them rehearse in little g-strings so he could better study their body movements. But always remember, Jack Cole never asked his dancers to do anything he couldn't do himself. Yet they didn't rebel because they knew something important was happening and they were happy to be part of it. They admired this strange man. They admired his talent and his artistry, and they understood him as well as anyone ever did. They were proud to be called a "Jack Cole dancer", which meant they were special.

Jack had a way of reaching dedicated, ambitious people without any problem. Look what he did with Rita Hayworth, Betty Grable and Marilyn Monroe. They no longer did the girly-girly dances. He gave them an identity. We can never forget Rita in *Put the Blame on Mame*, Betty in *No Talent Joe*, and Marilyn in *Diamonds are a Girl's Best Friend*. Jack was an anathema to the production departments of all studios, because he never met a budget. He ran over schedule and cost studios a lot of money. In fact, Darryl Zanuck once said, "He will never work here again." However, Darryl Zanuck had to contradict himself because Marilyn refused to work without him.

It has been said that Jack repeated himself. Well it's true. But we must remember, Jack was creating a new dance form. In ballet, people use and repeat the *tour jeté*, the *chaine* turns, the *pirouette*, the *arabesque*. In tap dancing, tap dancers use the wing, the buck and wing, the time step, soft-shoe, the riffs. Well Jack in his own way was creating new steps that no one else had done and he was always perfecting them, endlessly. Unfortunately, Jack, in a progression of his steps, developed a pattern that stayed with him and he could not move from it. And very often his steps were the same progression, whether it was a routine for Betty Grable or a routine for someone else. In fact, Betty once said to me that when Marilyn Monroe is up there dancing, Mitzi Gaynor or I could get on either side of her, we could join in without a rehearsal and go through the routine as well as she does. It was true. But Jack's dance vocabulary for his own work hadn't quite developed; it was at its very beginning. So he had to stick closely to home base, as it were. It took him ages to finish a dance combination.

I remember once when I was working on *Bloodhounds on Broadway* at Twentieth Century Fox with Mitzi Gaynor. Jack was working on a film with Marilyn Monroe and Yves Montand and there was a backstage sequence where Yves Montand was walking across the stage to visit Marilyn Monroe in her dressing room. While crossing, there were some dancers in the background warming up or doing some sort of exercise that dancers always do before they actually get out there and dance. But production wanted that choreographed and Jack took as much time to choreograph those few movements in the background, which would last only about eight bars of music, as the studio gave me to do one full, big number in *Bloodhounds on Broadway*.

Jack has given us excitement in dance as no one else before him had. He was a great contributor. He was an icon, as it were. He created a new art form of dance in the twentieth century. This man's influence on future dancers and choreographers is inestimable. They took his patterns, his new style of dance, ran with it and ran brilliantly. But without Jack there wouldn't have been this new form, this new dance form called "Modern Jazz". As Joe Tremaine, who is probably one of the best jazz dance teachers in our country, said, "If it hadn't been for Jack Cole, I would still be teaching the time-step." And that's true.

Jack was strange about the people who worked with him. He was proud of them but at the same time he didn't like any disloyalty to him or to his work. When he was in New York visiting, he went backstage at *Pajama Game* to visit Carol Haney, one of his pupils. He was very impressed with the number *Steam Heat*, which she really created even though she didn't get credit for it. He congratulated her and complimented her. He was very flattered because he saw his influence in her work. The next night however, he went to see *Damn Yankees* with Gwen Verdon. Well he was enraged. He told Gwen, "The numbers in this show are the best I have ever done." He never forgave Gwen for lifting his numbers "step by step" and giving them to another choreographer, Bob Fosse.

Jerome Robbins

Jerome Robbins was a product of the mid-1930s when pseudo-intellectuals roamed the streets of New York City's Greenwich Village, espousing any cause or joining any organization whose name ended in an "-ism." Modern dance companies were sprouting everywhere. Any unemployed, ham actor who could spell Stanislavsky opened a school to teach his method for acting.

In the late thirties, both Jerry Robbins and I were appearing on Broadway in a musical review called *Keep Off the Grass*. The show boasted such luminaries as Jimmy Durante, Ray Bolger, Betty Bruce, Jane Froman, Ilka Chase, Jackie Gleason, Emmet the Clown, Virginia O'Brien and Jose Limon. There were others in minor roles. In spite of this brilliant cast, the show was to close in two weeks. In *Keep Off the Grass*, George Balanchine choreographed a very amusing ballet. It was a spoof on cops and robbers, called *Jewel Thieves*. He designed the ballet for Ray Bolger and Betty Bruce. I danced a minor role in the ballet and Jerry Robbins was my understudy. Since the show was to close in two weeks, Jerry prevailed upon my love, my dear Betty Bruce, to talk me into letting him go on in my part, on the opening night, because his father was in the audience. I said, "Fine." The next night Betty came to me again and said, "Jerry's mother is in the audience, would you mind if he went on for you again?" I said, "All right." I stupidly agreed. And the third night, when Betty asked me to let Jerry dance because one of his distant cousins was coming, I cut her off and told her, "Hell no! I would like at least one member of my family to see me in this role before this turkey closes."

Backstage in the boy's dressing room, Jerry was always going on about politics. At the time, Hitler was on the move and he had just invaded or was on the verge of invading Poland. And so Jerry had something to shout about. He kept screaming, "Is the United States gonna stand by and watch the rape of Poland?" And one of the dancing boys in the dressing room said, "But Jerry, if the country does that, that means we're at war, we go to war." Jerry said, "Is your life worth more than the rape of Poland?" Of course, when the United States did get into the war to help Poland and the other countries, Jerry was the first one to waltz down to the draft hall and announce that he was gay, which meant of course that he could not serve in uniform.

Crazily enough, the Second World War did much for Jerry's career. Since many dancers were in uniform, Jerry had no competition. As a result, he advanced through the ranks of Ballet Theater and became a choreographer earlier than he might have if there had not been a war. But in all fairness to Jerry, it must be said that even then he had the talent and ability to be a choreographer.

Jerry's big break came when he staged the numbers for a musical called *High Button Shoes*. He conceived a ballet based on Mack Sennett characters at the beach. It was hysteria at its funniest. The critics raved about it. What the critics didn't know was that years earlier the Weidman-Humphrey Dance Company had a ballet in their repertoire called *Flickers*. Jerry actually was in it. And in *Flickers* there's a very similar beach scene with twenties costumes, beach costumes, the Keystone Cops. It was the one time in Jerry's career where his creativity was almost photographic. However, Jerry was wise enough to add Chaplinesque characters in this ballet, which gave it a freshness and new twist. At that time in Jerry's career, he did not see fit to thank the modern dancer Anna Sokolow for her help, nor acknowledge the Weidman-Humphrey Dance Company.

Politically, Jerry got into a serious mess when the "House Un-American Activities Committee" subpoenaed him. To get immunity for himself, he mentioned everyone he knew, best friends included, who might have carried Communist cards. Because of Jerry's betrayal of his friends he was really despised, many of his friends never speaking to him again.

Jerry came of age with his ballet *Fancy Free*. It was an immediate success. It had universal appeal to critics, audiences and the man on the street. They all loved the ballet. It had a light, music-hall quality to it and did a lot to change the concept of what the usually austere ballet could be. Because of this quality, it followed that Jerry would end up on Broadway, where he became the most important choreographer around. He did, strangely enough, become gracious for once in his life and mention people who had helped. For example, in *West Side Story*, he gave credit to Peter Gennaro, who really had done two of the good numbers in it, *America* being one. And so Peter's name appears on the program as a co-choreographer. He also gave credit to Yureka, who helped him immensely and danced the role in the *Uncle Tom Ballet* in *The King and I*.

Jerry's personality was chameleon-like. For some curious reason, he was very abusive to the Broadway dancer and the Broadway dancer does not hold still for that. The Gypsies really despised Jerry. They worked for him only because they needed the job. Otherwise they wouldn't have and openly told him so. Jerry's personality was strange, it was paranoia at its lowest. I think it had to do with Jerry's low self-esteem. Jerry really didn't like himself: he wished he had been taller, he didn't like his real name, he didn't like his background. He was a miserable soul and it's very unfortunate that someone with so much talent could be so despised. It would have been a different world for musical comedy if Jerome Robbins had been universally liked. But he wasn't, unfortunately. In every branch of the entertainment industry, people disliked this unfortunate man who possessed great, great talent.

Bob Fosse

In the world of entertainment, if there had been no Jack Cole, there wouldn't have been a Gwen Verdon. If there were no Gwen Verdon, there never would have been a Bob Fosse. I first met Bob Fosse and his charming wife, the amusing and wonderful Mary Ann Niles, when I was called in to doctor a musical review that was in trouble out of town before its Broadway run. They were a dance team in this musical, which was called *Dance Me a Song*. It was hopeless. There were twelve opening numbers, it was chi-chi, not the sort of fare that would make people want to come to the theatre. But in any case, I wanted to review the numbers and I asked everyone to show me what they had done for the show so far. Bob Fosse and Mary Ann Niles did their number for me. When it was finished, I told Fosse that the number lacked continuity, didn't flow properly and jumped around too much. He said, indignantly, "What do you mean? The first eight bars I took from Fred Astaire, the next eight bars Gene Kelly, and the next eight bars I took from Jack Cole — and I even took some tap steps from Ann Miller and Betty Bruce." So I told him, "That's exactly what's wrong with your number. You admire these people and so you imitate them and you're too literal." Then I said, "Always remember, inspiration is not imitation." That was a lesson I'm afraid Bob Fosse never learned.

In the show, I staged a number for Joan McCracken, she was one of the featured players, and Bobby Schearer. It was a typical boy-girl number, but I threw an amusing choice in and it worked well. But one night I noticed Bob Fosse standing in the wings and I thought he was envious, but that was not the case at all. He stood there with a red rose in his hand and as Joan McCracken came off the stage after a second bow, he handed it to her. That occurred the next night. And on the third night when I saw Fosse there I said to him, "What are you doing? You don't tell Joan McCracken she's a good dancer, she knows that." He said, "I'm not doing anything." Four weeks later Bob Fosse and Mary Ann Niles were divorced. Shortly after that, Bob Fosse and Joan McCracken were married.

Fosse was out of place in this new environment because Joan McCracken was a bit avant-garde and her friends were way out. And

Fosse basically was still a farm boy who had come to New York. Right before he left Joan McCracken, he got her to recommend him to the producers George Abbott and Bobby Fryer, so that he could choreograph their show *Pajama Game*. In *Pajama Game*, there was an outstanding number called *Steam Heat* that was danced by Carol Haney, Buzz Miller and Peter Gennaro. It stopped the show cold every night. It was no secret that Carol Haney and Buzz Miller, who both had been Jack Cole dancers, really set that number, Carol especially. Bob Fosse did add a few hat tricks, but the number basically was theirs, even though Carol never got credit for it officially.

At this point in his career, Fosse was always working. George Abbott signed him as choreographer for a new musical called *Damn Yankees*, starring Gwen Verdon. Here again, Gwen Verdon during rehearsals did her own numbers and did them rather well. Because she had been, earlier in her career, an assistant to Jack Cole on most of his films and she had a wealth of material, Jack Cole's material, to fall back on. Bob Fosse and Gwen Verdon became very friendly and soon after that they were married. They made a very exciting and successful team. Unfortunately, Fosse began to look for other women, especially those that might be of help to him. Bob Fosse had a very special talent. He could take someone else's idea or routine and add his own panache to it and the result would be exciting. And that's what a good director does really. A director is not necessarily creative. A choreographer is creative. The lyricist and composer are creative. The scenic designer is creative. The costume designer is creative. But a good director takes all these elements, blends them together, takes what he wants from each one of them and the result is a successful play. And that is what Fosse could do beautifully. He proved that when he took the stage version of *Cabaret* and transposed it to film. The result was electrifying. It was a tremendous hit. He did have that talent.

He had the potential to become one of the most successful directors on Broadway. But, unfortunately, with success came bad habits. He drank too much, he smoked too much, he caroused around too much. What might have been a very exciting musical comedy world with his contribution as director was wiped out because Bob Fosse left us at the very height of his career.

Robert Sidney

The Divas

Robert Sidney

Lily Pons

When I was asked to do a number for Lily Pons and Danny Kaye for the ANTA (American National Theatre Authority) Ball, I thought the idea of pairing these two unlikely artists together doing a duet had unlimited possibilities. I knew Danny Kaye would love that concept; however, I wondered whether the world's most wonderful coloratura, Lily Pons, would share our enthusiasm. Danny and I both arrived at her home in Silvermine, Connecticut, where she greeted us at the door and said, "Before we do business, we have lunch first. I have a very special dish for you from my native Marseilles. We call it *Allouette Sans Tete.*" The *allouette* being a little sparrow-like bird, the *sans tete* meaning without a head. (Really it's just rolled beef with a toothpick in it to hold it together). But Danny pounced on *allouette*. He immediately went into a five minute bit on the old nursery rhyme "Allouette, gentille allouette..." He sang it in his fractured French, then he murdered it in his Italian double-talk. Then he went into German. Lily Pons was hysterical. She could not contain her laughter. As a matter of fact she tried to sing with him.

We didn't have a rehearsal pianist, but Lily's celebrated conductor husband, Andre Kostelanetz, volunteered to help. Unfortunately, the piano is not his instrument. So, our accompaniment was a finger-plucking piano.

The number we ended up with, I must admit, was really funny. Lily and Danny entered from either side of the stage with great pomp and circumstance, came center-stage, bowed to the audience, bowed to each other. Then Danny indicated with great flourish that Lily should step forward and sing. She sang one of the trills from The Bell Song from *Lakme*. Then Lily indicated that Danny come forward and do his bit. He came forward with great majesty and with great stance, took the deepest breath, and all he did was burp and step back. Then Lily took over again with another trill. And then she indicated that it was Danny's turn again. He stepped forward, cleared his throat and tried to make a sound. But nothing came out and he stepped back. Then Lily came forward and sang really quite a long section of the aria from *Lakme*, then indicated for Danny to come forward. He did, and he went into a crazy scat and repeated his scat music, which at the time was very popular. Actually, the scat music you could call the precursor of modern rap music, the difference being that scat had style, dignity and good taste, unlike modern rap. Anyway, Danny went on with his scat thing and Lily improvised an obligato against it. And the two together went into some wild dance steps and brought the house down. It really was outstanding and couldn't have been funnier. Lily Pons exhibited a comedic sense one never suspected she had.

Right before they went on stage to do their duet, Lily came to me and said, "I know I shall sing really good tonight because I just threw up." Fortunately, opera stars only do two performances a week. I'd hate to think what would happen to Lily Pons if she had to sing eight performances, as they do on Broadway.

Leontyne Price

Of all the guests we had on the Pearl Bailey television show, one of my favorites was the exquisite soprano Leontyne Price. Her rendition of *Un Bel Di* still sends me into a musical trance. Leontyne chose to sing an aria from *La Forza del Destino* on our show, which is really opera at its heaviest. Our poor theatre orchestra had a rough time keeping up with the music. But valiantly they struggled and valiantly they won. The divine Leontyne never complained once about her musical background. It all worked out magically. The audience really enjoyed hearing opera at its finest.

There was a section of *The Pearl Bailey Show* that was neither rehearsed nor scripted. It was totally improvised. It was Pearl interviewing her guests, who were at the mercy of her mood at the time. Pearl told the audience that Leontyne had sung *Oh Promise Me* at Pearl's wedding to Louie Belson, the famous drummer, while Leontyne was appearing in *Porgy and Bess* in London. Without any warning, she asked Leontyne to sing *Oh Promise Me* for the audience. Leontyne glowered at Pearl, walked to the footlights and said, "Hit it, Louie!" She went into a chorus of *Oh Promise Me*. Pearl Bailey was sitting nearby at a table with a tambourine at her side. And she kept supplying rhythm as a background, although nobody asked her to. You see, Pearl loved her fellow performers, especially when they weren't performing. The little tambourine got louder and louder, and Leontyne kept singing louder and louder. When it got to the second chorus, she said "Pearl, this is your turn." Pearl got up and couldn't wait for the moment she was going to sing. She started to sing *Oh Promise Me* and when she did Leontyne took that tambourine and with the solemn dignity of a Salvation Army lass, went through the audience asking for alms for the poor. Well it broke up the place. The audience was hysterical. Even Pearl fell on the floor crying with laughter – she couldn't catch her breath. The two of them sang the second half of the song together. To this very day when I'm at a wedding ceremony, at that solemn moment when someone starts to sing *Oh Promise Me*, I rush for the nearest exit, hoping I can get out in time before I ruin the ceremony.

Patrice Munsell

I was busy working on some dance patterns with my assistant, Wisa D'Orso, when I had an S.O.S. call from Lee Hale, our vocal director on The Dean Martin Show, who was having a problem with one of our guest performers. I rushed over to his rehearsal hall and there was a very formidable looking young woman, heavily furred and very, very grand. She said, "Who's this?" Lee said, "This is our choreographer, Bob Sidney." And she said, "Oh? And I suppose you expect me to dance, too?" To which I replied, "I never expect small favors from anyone." And with that she threw off her coat and she was fully dressed in a leotard ready for rehearsal. This divine character was Patrice Munsell, the American-born opera star. The booking agent told her that she was to sing Strauss on *The Dean Martin Show*. Naturally, she assumed that she was going to sing *Die Fleidermaus* or some other opera by Strauss. Instead, she was told the song by Strauss that she was going to sing was George Gershwin's *By Strauss*. That was the reason for the pretended outburst of temperament.

I must say that I never enjoyed rehearsals more than I did with Patrice Munsell. She was a joy to work with. For an opera star, she never took herself too seriously and was always good for a laugh. One day, she arrived for rehearsal wearing heavily jewelled star sapphire bracelets – apparently she had an important engagement after rehearsal. I said, "You don't expect to dance with all that hardware you have on, do you?" She took the bracelets off, threw them at me and said, "Here, take care of the hardware. If something happens to it, I'll own you for the next 10 years of your life."

She loved the dance portion of the song, especially when she was lifted by the male dancers. The guys would lift her and throw her around and she went through it all like a pro. In the camera long shots, people thought we had a double dancing for Patrice, but she did the whole number herself. I thought she was brilliant.

Also, during breaks she would sit and talk to the ladies. In fact, she once told Wisa D'Orso, "I'll never understand why people make such a big deal about the pain, suffering and pushing of childbirth. All I do is hit a high C and out comes the baby!"

I'm sure that every time Patrice Munsell sings *Die Fleidermaus* at the opera, she misses being thrown around by her dancing boys.

Hollywood Imports

Ann-Margret

I always thought Ann-Margret was an American. Not so! She hails from Sweden, as did two other exceptional Imports – Greta Garbo and Ingrid Bergman. When Ann-Margret arrived in the States, she was young enough to have been absorbed by our teenybopper culture. Fortunately, she came through unscathed.

I first worked with Ann-Margret on a film for Twentieth Century Fox Studios called *Pleasure Seekers*. Most of it was shot on location in Spain. We were filming in Madrid, when I had a visitor to our set – Clint Eastwood. I knew Clint from the States. He was very depressed and invited me to his apartment at the Torre de Madrid, a hotel right near where we were working. He was there with his wife and apparently he had just finished his last "Spaghetti Western," which were the pictures produced in Italy on a shoestring under very difficult conditions. And since they didn't gross much and he had just finished his last picture, he said he was giving up the business, going back to the States and doing something quite different. Fortunately, this last Spaghetti Western was a tremendous hit, and when Clint did go back to the States he did it at a fantastic salary and made very important Westerns from then on.

We had another visitor to the set. The publicity department arranged for the famous bullfighter El Cordobes to come and greet Ann-Margret. He was instructed to bow in a very courtly manner and say some words in Spanish that would mean "I welcome you, or I salute you, my great beauty." Also, he was told that Ann-Margret was a redhead. He arrived on the set and before anyone could prompt him, he went over, bowed low and said his greeting in Spanish. But he was not addressing Ann-Margret: he was talking to the wardrobe woman, who had red hair.

We had locations in Marbella and in Estapona that we liked because we got to work with real Spanish gypsies. They were quite taken with Ann-Margret because she was a redhead and they think that's quite beautiful. And she is beautiful. The male gypsies especially were most attentive. They never missed a rehearsal and never missed a take in front of the camera. The female gypsies were different: we had to run and find them because if they got bored they just would leave.

We had one location back in the States and Ann-Margret was to do this number with Antonio Gardes, the foremost flamenco dancer in Spain. It was a very nice routine and we were apprehensive because we thought perhaps he would look down on our dancing. On the contrary, he was most complimentary and he worked very hard with Ann-Margret. The number they did turned out to be quite exciting. We also had the advantage of his guitarist, who was one of the best in the world. Ann-Margret, because of her energy and her excitement, did remarkably well dancing with this incredible artist.

Ann-Margret is a very dedicated performer, the sort of lady who without fuss gets the job done, and I admire her for that.

Joan Collins

In the musical film *The Opposite Sex*, Joan Collins played the part of a scheming, conniving, aggressive chorus girl, who manages to take the producer away from his wife, played by June Allyson. In the script, June's character is also in show business. She's a star. The authors of the script thought that it was wise to have Joan Collins dance, since she was to play the part of a chorine. However, they never bothered to ask if she *could* dance. She couldn't.

Once again, I had to do what I did with Susan Hayward. I managed to create something that Joan could do, to camouflage the fact that she wasn't a dancer. It wasn't as difficult as it was in Susan's case, because in the number Joan was to appear, she was one of four girl dancers who were a background for comedian Dick Shawn. I had no problems with Joan. She tried her best, and I did my best to make her feel good. She knew that, and we got along very well.

This particular number was done very early in the shooting schedule. As the movie progressed, Joan suddenly realized that she had a very important part and she began to spread her wings. There's a scene in the film in which June Allyson is confronted by Joan, who taunts her, reminding her that June's character has lost her husband because she "didn't know how to hold on to a man." The scene called for June to slap her.

Cameras started rolling, everything went fine until it was time for June to slap Joan. June broke down. She cried and was really hysterical because, as she explained it, "I've never slapped anyone. I just can't do it." The director talked to her, saying she had to do it because it was part of the script. They tried it again and the same thing happened. It was time for June's slap and she broke down again.

Joan, completely forgetting that June was the star of the film, said, "Oh, come off it. We've had enough of this drama. Let's get on with it. Just slap me and get the whole damn thing over with." They rolled the film again, and June slapped Joan so hard that Joan's hairpiece flew off her head.

Later in Joan Collins' career, when she played one of the leads in that wonderful television series *Dynasty*, there were many members of that cast who would have gladly slapped her, even if the script didn't call for it. Joan played the part of a bitch, but unfortunately some of her fellow actors felt that she played her part too convincingly, especially off the camera.

<u>Elke Sommer</u>

Elke Sommer is one of the most guileless beauties one could ever hope to meet. She's so totally honest it's almost frightening. She just says what she thinks – it doesn't matter where she is or to whom she is talking. She's absolutely incredible. I remember the first time I met her she was to appear on *The Dean Martin Show*. Wisa D'Orso, my assistant, and I were working on a number for Elke, who was a little late. Suddenly Elke came tearing into the studio, wearing a sort of a beaded band around her head and a see-through blouse. I knew she spoke French and I was told by one of my friends that she was a delight, so I said to her in French, "How dare you come late and how dare you wear that slutty blouse?" She answered in French, saying "You Americans make me (expletive omitted here). You invent a see-through blouse and then you make an issue about it when someone's wearing it. So very well, off it comes." And she starts to take the blouse off and she's entirely naked. Every male on the floor at the studio of NBC seemed to pop into our rehearsal hall all at once. We restored her to decency, covered her, and went on with the number.

She sang the Maurice Chevalier song called *Thank Heaven for Little Girls*. Except Elke sang it as *Thank Heaven for Little Boys*. She did this number on a polar bear rug with four of our male dancers. How it ever passed the censors I never knew. Yet it was quite innocent. There wasn't one indecent movement in it, but it was all innuendo and she's an expert at that.

After that number, she and Dean Martin did their duet together on that same rug. There was much rolling around on that rug. It really became a contest to see who could outdo the other. Curiously enough we did get complaints from animal lovers saying how dare we deface a polar bear, how dare we kill. Actually, they were trying to say the number was shocking. But all they had the nerve to complain about was the poor polar bear, which had been dead for a long time.

I remember once at a party, Elke was explaining to some people a method for proper breathing and this one gentleman didn't quite understand her. So she said, "Put your hand here," and she took his hand and put it right under her breast by her diaphragm. As he was still confused (frankly I think he was leading her on), she quite innocently said "No, no, here" and immediately off came her slacks. She started to take her blouse off and I said, "Elke, not again please!" But she kept going. The poor man who was egging her on was embarrassed and he said, "I understand, you don't have to explain anymore." She was a delight to be with.

I knew that Elke was a brilliant sculptress and a good painter. One day I asked her if I could buy one of her paintings. She said, "Well, come to the house and choose one." She told me her address; it was in one of the canyons. I went there, rang the doorbell; no one answered. Finally, I saw this young man painting or mending the roof and I yelled up to him, "Where is Elke Sommer, Mrs. Joe Hyams?" She was married at that time to Joe Hyams, the writer. "Where is Ms. Sommer?" She took the cap off her head and said, "Here I am, can't you see? I'm trying to do something. I'm fixing the roof!" She came down, we saw her paintings and then I chose one I liked especially. When I tried to pay for the painting, she said, "Don't be silly, that's your Christmas present." I protested, but she insisted upon it.

One day at the studio, several of us were having a serious talk. She gave us her impressions of being a little girl of three or four when we were bombing Germany during World War II. It was very sad, very pathetic. This little child frightened by the terror in the skies and suddenly you realize, it didn't matter which side was bombing the other. What did matter was that little children were being exposed to the horror and cruelty of war.

I hear from Elke every Christmas. I get either a print of one of her works of art or a sweet card. There so much one could learn from an Elke Sommer, her honesty, which knows no bounds, and her directness, which strikes wherever it has to, and her love, which is constant.

Hermione Gingold

I was at a smart restaurant on 52nd Street having lunch with Nora Kaye, the American ballerina, when I heard a woman's booming voice from across the restaurant. I knew immediately that such volume could only be the voice of Hermione Gingold. So I called the waiter over and I wrote a little note that simply said, "Hermione, if it's you, I'm here, Bob Sidney with a friend. I'd like to say hello." He brought the note to Hermione's table. She read it, got up and started to shout, "Bob Sidney, where is he? Where is Bob Sidney?" It was so loud you thought she was introducing a sporting event at Madison Square Garden.

Hermione was a dear friend of mine in England during the Blitz when *This Is The Army*, the Irving Berlin soldier show, played there. We were fed and treated beautifully by many of the English theatrical colony and Hermione took me under her wing. She and I shared an interest in English Staffordshire. She was appearing with Hermione Baddeley in Noel Coward's, *Fallen Angels*. The two ladies were hysterical. They were really funny. One tried to outdo the other. Actually, the ladies despised each other, but you'd never know it onstage, they played so brilliantly.

After we finished our show and after Hermione finished hers, she often would meet me at The Ivy, a restaurant that was very popular with people in the theater. Even though the bombs were dropping all around, you'd never know it with the way that the English calm prevailed. Every time a bomb dropped it was ignored completely. One particular night, this man came in and Hermione said, "Don't turn around just yet, I'll tell you when, but somebody just came in you must hear about." I said, "Who is it?" I thought it was another English celebrity. She said, "No, he's a German spy." I said, "Hermione, but it doesn't make sense, if he's a spy, how can he be walking around without being detected, without being sequestered, or arrested?" She said, "No, no, we don't do things the way you Americans do." I said, "But it makes no sense, he's a spy, he's a threat, he's a danger." She said, "On the contrary. We like to see him walking around and watch what he's doing. That's the only way we can keep up with his machinations. Then, when the time is right, we'll arrest him." I thought she was totally mad, but then I realized that it made good sense. If the minute he appeared someone did arrest him, that would be the end of his mission.

Hermione also invited me one night to her house on Kinnerton Street. Somehow she managed to prepare a delicious dish, even though eggs, milk and other foods were almost impossible to find in England. I was so happy to finally taste something that vaguely resembled home cooking. The doorbell rang and in came three of her friends. Of course Hermione had to invite them to join us and they did. Although there was not quite enough food to go around, we managed nevertheless. Suddenly, we heard a bomb drop and one of the guests went out the door to look and said, "Oh do come. It's the most lovely fire we've had this week." That was the English attitude. I admired the calm. The Nazis could send over as many bombs as they cared to, but somehow or other they would never disturb the English calm, a quality I've admired ever since in the English people.

When Hermione Gingold got to the States to do *Gigi*, I thought it was my duty to return the kindness she had showed me. As often as I could, I would meet her, escort her to the studio, do anything to please her. In *Gigi*, Hermione played opposite Maurice Chevalier. When you see the film it's a lovely relationship between the two of them. But, actually, off-screen they didn't get along at all. He found Hermione's voice unmusical and irritating. She thought his accent was disturbingly affected. When the film was released it was a tremendous hit and naturally most of the stars were interviewed by the press. In one interview Hermione gave, they asked her how it felt to work opposite Maurice Chevalier. She said that it was the realization of a dream she'd always had – to play a scene with the idol of France. A gentleman, with such gallantry, such wit, such humor. She said it was an experience she would never forget. When her friends asked her about this interview and her complimentary remarks about Chevalier, she said, "It's the best performance I ever gave in my life."

Gina Lollobrigida

Gina Lollobrigida was one of the guests on *The Dean Martin Show*. On her first appearance, the producer insisted, as usual, that she do a musical number. She hoped she would do a sketch with Dean to show that she was a good actress, which she was. We did a number and fortunately she could move a little bit, although this was not her *forté*. She did have a pleasant voice however, so we used it to it's fullest, with the boys behind her doing most of the dancing work. It came off quite nicely. She was pleased.

The second time she came back she was treated very rudely. Our producer treated her as if she were an extra. For some reason, he didn't honor his promise that she was not going to have to do another musical number. She said she was not a musical performer but a dramatic actress. She was right and her reasoning was intelligent. It got to a point where it became extremely unpleasant. Poor Dean Martin had nothing to do with this, he didn't even know about it. He was in his dressing room. He hadn't come out yet because no one had called him to do what he was supposed to do with her, which was really very little. Suddenly she got on the phone and spoke with her lawyer or her agent, and then refused to do anything until the company gave her a certified check in the amount of $7,000, which was the top fee we gave visiting artists. It was a "Favored Nations" clause, which means that is the established ongoing price.

I was embarrassed because the woman was in another country, our country, and I felt we had a responsibility to treat her the way we would like to be treated in her country. And she did say, almost prophetically, that if anyone like Dean Martin or anyone connected with our staff ever showed up in Italy and tried to work there, they would never have a chance to because she would have them blacklisted. The woman was upset and I'm sure she never forgave our producer's bad manners.

Zsa Zsa Gabor

When Zsa Zsa Gabor was on *The Dean Martin Show* she was very upset and I asked her why. She said, "My poor sister Magda had a stroke you know and her husband, he's a beast, he's so mean, he's so cruel, he doesn't help her at all, this dreadful man." And I said, "Oh, I'm so sorry Zsa Zsa." A few months later she appeared on the show again and this time she was upset once more and I said, "What's wrong now Zsa Zsa?" She said, "My sveet dahling, my sveet, sveet, dahling brother-in-law. My brother-in-law he just died." I said, "Zsa Zsa, you told me he was a cruel man." She said, "How dare you say that? He left her $18,000,000!"

One day, she invited me to her house to discuss directing a nightclub act for her because she had seen some of the acts I had done for other people. I tried desperately to explain to her that she was a unique performer who did what no other performer could do. She could talk and answer questions, which was wonderful. I did go to see her act and it was very non-traditional. As I said, it was questions and answers, but they were funny. In fact, I remember someone in the audience asked her, "I've just broken off my engagement. Shall I return the ring?" She said, "Well of course dahling, you must return the ring to the man. Only keep the diamond." I said, "Zsa Zsa, if you do an act like that it will be wonderful."

In any case, she gave me lunch and kept offering me wine. Finally after the second glass I said, "No, no more." But I noticed that she hadn't touched her wine, or the liquor. We were interrupted because we heard all this noise. I said, "What's going on up there?" She said, "It's my sister Eva. She's jealous because I am having an interview about a nightclub act and she's teasing my daughter Francesca." I said, "Well that's terrible of her!" She said, "How dare you speak about my sister like that?" That was a typical Gaborism.

As we were talking she had this tray of wonderful pastries – éclairs and all the sorts of things that you shouldn't eat. She'd say, "Sveetheart, dahling, won't you have one?" I said, "No thank you." And she kept feeding these éclairs to her dog, a big standard poodle. Finally, I said, in exasperation, "Zsa Zsa, do you realize you must not feed sweets to a dog?" She said, "Why?" I said, "Because it's not good for them." She said, "Let me ask you a question sveetheart, dahling. How long can this breed of dog usually live?" I said, "All things being equal, a poodle could live to be around 14 years old." She said, "Well wouldn't you rather live and die at 13 years old knowing that you tasted all the best things in life, all the joy and the delights in life, all the delicacies in life, than to die at the age of 14 not ever having experienced any of this?" I got to thinking that she had a very interesting theory. It sure was the philosophy that Zsa Zsa Gabor and all the Gabors lived by. It does make sense though. It may be a little hedonistic, but even then, why shouldn't one enjoy life to it's fullest instead of waiting in an armchair for the end to come?

The Sinatras

Frank Sinatra

I had just finished directing the Sonja Henie ice show, when I was signed by Howard Hughes, who at that time was the sole owner of RKO Studios, to stage the musical numbers in the film *Susan Slept Here*, starring Dick Powell and a newcomer, Debbie Reynolds. I had hoped I could have a few days between assignments to catch my breath, because the Sonja Henie ice show was a nightmare. But unfortunately I was told I had to be at the airport that night to catch the midnight flight to the Coast, which would get me there in the morning. I arrived at the airport and all the TWA agents treated me with great respect, as if I was a visiting potentate. And I realized why. Howard Hughes owned TWA. In fact one agent made a great point of telling me that he was able to remove a passenger from the sleeping berth and I was to take that berth for myself. I thanked him. I was on the plane and was waiting for it to take off when on came Frank Sinatra and Ava Gardner, his wife at that time. He was in an ugly mood and I heard him say, "I'd like to find that son of a bitch who had me bumped off my sleeping berth." When Frank was angry he was known to throw a few punches and I certainly didn't want to be around for that performance. So I slid down in my seat as far as I could go, hoping not to be noticed. Of course, it didn't occur to me then that Frank Sinatra didn't know who I was, but I was taking no chances.

I kept thinking about an incident involving Frank that happened in Hawaii when he was on location with *From Here To Eternity*, in which he played a supporting role but did win the Oscar for his performance. He was in his dressing room, I was told, very unhappy and very forlorn because his marriage to Ava was on the rocks, when one of his assistants came to his room and said, "They're ready for you on the set so you'd better get moving, shake a leg, get to it, on the double," or something like that. Frank didn't particularly appreciate the familiarity and so he hauled off and hit the kid so hard he flew out of the dressing room door. When the director Fred Zinneman heard about the incident, he immediately called Hollywood and informed the top brass that if Sinatra didn't shape up and another incident like the one in the dressing room happened again, Sinatra would be fired or Fred Zinneman would quit the picture.

When I thought the coast was clear, I moved from my hiding place on the plane and tip-toed to the sleeping section of the cabin. As I passed Sinatra, I couldn't help but notice that he, with Ava in his arms, was sleeping soundly with a big smile on his face. When I got to my berth in the sleeping area, I was so exhausted emotionally I just fell on the bed, shoes and all, and fell asleep. Suddenly, the stewardess, who apparently thought I was an important executive with TWA or RKO Studios, woke me. She whispered to me confidentially that we were having engine trouble and would have to make a forced landing in Chicago. At that point I was distraught. I thought, "What could happen next? Frank Sinatra's temper and rage or the plane about to crash?" There was nothing I could do about it. It was like a black comedy. I did the only thing I could – I fell asleep.

I got to work with Frank Sinatra on a television special – a shortened version of Cole Porter's musical *Anything Goes.* Frank and Ethel Merman starred in the production. I thought that was very strange casting, because Frank looked like Ethel's son, hardly her leading man. Rehearsals ran very smoothly. Frank was adored by everyone there, especially the girl dancers, which made Frank very happy. He and Ethel got along very well. Except, I must say, that I expected him to balk at the way she performed. Unlike Frank, who plays a scene by relating to the person opposite him, Ethel only relates to the spotlight in front. She stands in one position and belts those songs out in her own inimitable style and never moves from that spot.

I thought Frank would raise objections about her technique – it's not easy to play with someone who doesn't respond to you – but he didn't. He behaved nicely. In fact he was amused and intrigued by it. Once he got the form it never shook him one bit. Finally, he said to me, "I've got an idea." I asked him what it was and he replied, "You know when you do the number *You're the Top* and you stage it, put a little dance number in there and that will make her move from one spot. Give her some business where she has to move, and I'll be dancing up a storm." In fact, believe it or not, Frank could dance. Because, even though he denied it, in the movie *Anchors Aweigh*, he and Gene Kelly, dressed as sailors, did a number together. Frank held up very nicely against Gene. So, I thought, "Why not? In this instance we'll do a number with a little movement in it." Ethel went along with it. However, as she moved, she kept looking out front and never changed her position one bit. Frank, on the other hand, was delightful. He played it like an imp. He improvised gestures. He improvised takes, double takes and triple takes. He was absolutely charming. He really made the number. It was a show stopper.

When the shoot came to an end, I thanked all the dancing people first. I always do, because they are the most important in my world. Then I thanked the crew, then Ethel and some of the principals. I went by to thank Frank but his dressing room was full of visitors, mostly his cronies. I shouted, "Frank, bye, I'll see you later." He came tearing out in the hall in his undershorts. (Frank Sinatra in his undershorts was quite a sight!) He said, "Where are you going? You stop! Aren't you going to say goodbye?" And he hugged me and couldn't have been nicer. I said, "Frank, you better get back to your room. You're in your shorts. You're exposing yourself." "Oh relax," he said. "They all know about it anyway." I must say, Frank impressed me tremendously on that show. He was a great, great artist, in or out of his shorts.

I had done an act for Joey Heatherton and she had played Caesar's Palace several times with Frank as the headliner. But they talked her into opening for Frank in this instance, which we did. Joey's act usually took at least an hour, but all they wanted from us this time was thirty minutes. So we pruned the act to thirty minutes and it went fine. We were rehearsing on the stage when some stage manager there who was apparently timing our act said, "You know, you went over twenty minutes. You're only supposed to do twenty minutes." I said, "No, that's not in our contract. We're to have thirty minutes." He said "No". We were arguing when in came Frank, and he said, "What's wrong, kid?" I said, "Mr. Sinatra..." And he said, "When will you call me Frank?" So I said, "OK, Frank, we have a problem. This guy insists that we're only to do twenty minutes. We were told to do thirty minutes and we can't possibly make another change in the act." With that, he said to the stage manager, "Get lost. And don't you ever bother these nice people again. You take all the time you need." I thought that was gracious of him.

Then he met Joey and liked her very much. He invited us to watch his orchestra rehearsal, which we did. They started playing his music and he stopped them after two bars and said, "There's a wrong note someplace. Do it again." They did it again and he stopped them again

74

and said, "No, no. That wrong note's still there." The musicians were apprehensive because they knew he was about to explode. Again he said, "Do it again. And again." Finally, I said to Joey, "Let's get going, because he's about to blow a fuse." In spite of Sinatra's temper, he was a great artist and a gracious artist. He treated other performers with respect. You can't but help admire this man.

I suspect one of Frank's greatest theatrical experiences was the gala that Gregory Peck produced for the industry for the benefit of the Motion Picture Home. This was also to honor Frank, since this was going to be his farewell performance. I was chosen by Gregory Peck to be his Associate Producer and I was very flattered by that honor. Because you can't do it all by yourself. I must say up front that Gregory Peck is the most gentle of gentlemen. He is the kindest soul. Sometimes you wonder what he is doing in show business.

Anyway, we worked very hard. It was a well-planned show. We had to arrange rehearsal schedules for the different performers, because some of them were appearing in shows elsewhere and could only come the day of the event, which was on a Sunday. Things were going along comparatively smoothly in spite of all this hectic activity, until we had one unfortunate incident. Barbra Streisand's manager informed Mr. Peck that he was to come to Ms. Streisand's home. They wanted to discuss a few things before she would commit herself to the show. Gregory took me along. I knew he was very upset and very worried. We arrived and she was very gracious. Her manager took over immediately, saying: "Now look, Ms. Streisand is to have the same length of performance time as Mr. Sinatra. Also, she will decide where in the program she will appear. Also, and most importantly, the orchestra rehearsal has to be done at her convenience."

I could tell that poor Gregory was perplexed and didn't know what to say. So I jumped in and I told this manager, "Now look, you must bear one thing in mind. We are most eager to have Ms. Streisand on the show because she probably will be the big hit of the evening. However, you must also appreciate that we are doing this as a benefit for the Motion Picture Home and it is to be Frank Sinatra's farewell performance. We don't regard this as a competition or as a popularity contest. We regard this as a contribution to the industry that has been very kind to all of us." With that, Barbra Streisand, who I suspect is really as clever a business woman as she is a brilliant artist, spoke up and said, "There's no problem. We'll be there and it will all work out beautifully."

And it did work out beautifully. Every conceivable artist appeared on that show. Even Princess Grace left her throne in Monaco to be with Frank. I watched Frank; he was in the wings. He was almost teary-eyed. He was very impressed and really flattered. When he came on stage, the applause was thunderous. It was an ovation the sort of which he never got when he was on his own in a nightclub. It was a wonderful moment in the theater and deservedly so, because Frank Sinatra was one of our great artists and he will always remain an icon of popular music.

Nancy Sinatra

Nancy Sinatra's first time out as a recording artist broke all records. She made the top 10 in *Billboard*, the showbiz bible, and she stayed in the top 10 for three or four months. She became an instant celebrity and appeared on many talk shows. When she played the Dean Martin show, we on the production staff didn't quite know what to do with her. After all, she was Frank Sinatra's little girl. The first day of rehearsal I was really surprised. We were waiting for Nancy Sinatra and there she was, sitting in the back of the hall at least twenty minutes before any of us got there. She wanted no special favors because she was Frank's daughter. She got along with the gypsies; and when the female gypsies like you, you're in. Before the first day of rehearsal had ended, she knew every dancer by his or her first name. They loved her.

Nancy seriously asked me if she would have to do *These Boots Were Made for Walkin*? I said that I was afraid they would want her to. So, I said, "I promise you, Nancy, we'll try to do something different." She said, "OK, I trust you." And we did do something different. Nancy was out there on the stage all alone singing *Boots*, but very fluidly. We had all the girl dancers in a straight row, so all you saw was Nancy. At a certain point, legs came out, arms came out, and finally they all came out and there was an army of girls doing *Boots* with Nancy. That was the finale of the song. Sounds corny, but it worked very nicely. Nancy was very grateful.

In fact, several months later she asked if I would work with her on a new medium called Colorsonics. Actually, it was a jukebox that had a built-in screen. When you chose a record, you'd hear the music and then on the screen would be the visual interpretation of it. It was just like being at home with your own TV set, except that you put a quarter in to hear a particular record. We had to do *Boots*, but we did it very seriously, very straightforwardly. No tricks. On the other side of the record, she chose to sing *The Shadow of Your Smile*. We thought we might give it a little background. Nancy suggested, "Why don't we put it at a seashore. There's something so beautiful about water and sand and people in bathing suits." I said, "Good idea, Nancy. Bring a bathing suit." She appeared the next day when we were ready to shoot *The Shadow of Your*

Smile and she had this bathing suit under her arm. She asked me, "What do you think?" I said, "Looks good. Looks great." I was too busy with the lighting at that point. She appeared on the set and I almost fell over. She was wearing the shortest bikini I had seen on anyone. I said, "Nancy, what is that?" She said, "It's a bikini." I said, "If you mother knew I had anything to do with this, she'd kill me." Nancy said, "Nonsense. Mother picked this bikini."

Nancy Sinatra wanted to present herself as another type than the girl next door. It would help her career. And understandably, when she did the centerfold in *Playboy*, I wasn't shocked. A lot of people in the business weren't shocked either. She wasn't the first celebrity, incidentally, to appear in *Playboy*. But in Nancy's case, she did it because she wanted to break from her image and show different sides of herself. And there's no better place than *Playboy* to show different sides of anyone.

Frank Sinatra, Jr.

When Frank Sinatra, Jr. appeared at the rehearsal hall of the Dean Martin summer show *The Golddiggers*, it looked as if he were in the wrong place. His general manners suggested a scholarly philosophy student with thesis in hand, on his way to the review board for his doctorate. But as it turned out, he really was in the right place.

It was the first day reading *The Golddiggers* and I introduced him to everyone there: Paul Lynde, a uniquely talented comedian whose sneer is more devastating than a stick of TNT; Joey Heatherton, whose sexuality just oozes from her – if she were wearing a nun's habit she would look sexy; a comedienne named Barbara Heller, who was deeply engrossed in her script because she was terrified of Paul Lynde; and The Golddiggers, who did their own numbers and were also involved with the sketches now and then.

We sat down and began to read the sketches. I could see Frank's face turn white. Apparently, he wasn't ready for this and he was terrified. It was quite obvious to me, and I suddenly realized that this must not go on. Paul was reading his part and he had a long soliloquy. Suddenly I stopped and said, "Here's Lee Hale, our Music Director. It's very important we get the proper vocal keys for all of us here. So we'll have to do that now and we'll take a break later." And we did. We got keys and broke for lunch and then everybody left. Frank came over and said, "I want to thank you for what you've done." It was a tacit understanding between us. I suggested that I would help in any way I could and he appreciated this. I actually got to teach him how to make an entrance on stage and how to make an exit. Most performers don't know how and when to get off the stage.

Frank worked out beautifully. As the season progressed he improved with each show. By the end of the little series he was a solid performer. After the show he went out with his orchestra. Frank's love really is music. He loves the band and traveling with the band. He's really a musicologist. He has a very good sense and knowledge of music.

For example, Frank Sr. did stop the orchestra when they played the first two bars of the introduction because there was a wrong note someplace. He didn't know where, but he knew there was a wrong note and he was right. Frank Jr. would not only say there was a wrong note, he'd tell you the instrument and who played it. He had as much respect for the haunting oboe as he did for the wailing saxophone.

He loved to conduct. In fact, one of his great moments was when he conducted for his father on stage and did a very good job. Unfortunately, sometimes when he's out there singing on his own, he forgets himself and conducts the orchestra, which I think is strange.

I expected a lot from Frank Jr. and still do. I was very disappointed when his father died – we all were – but I was hoping he would carry on the tradition or would wear his father's mantle. He had everything to justify that. It was not just someone taking his father's place because it was his father – Frank was able to do it. But unfortunately I always had the feeling that Frank had that "He's my father syndrome" that hampers many young performers. They want to be independent. They don't want people to recognize them because of their parents. I think Frank is a strong advocate of that. It's a shame, because I think he's the only one who could succeed his famous, wonderful father, and it's sad that he doesn't see it that way. However, I do have great respect for him as a person. Frank Sinatra, Jr. is bright, intelligent and a good musician, who also sings beautifully. He has everything going for him and I wish him all the luck in the world.

Members of the Irving Berlin World War II all-soldiers show *This Is The Army.* © Warnecke and Cranston.

In uniform with Irving Berlin on the Warner Brothers set during the filming of the *Yip, Yip, Yaphank* sequence of *This Is The Army*. © Warner Brothers.

Directing the troops with Warner Brothers director Michael Curtiz on *This Is The Army.* © Warner Brothers.

With Rita Hayworth on *The Loves of Carmen*. © Columbia Pictures Corp.

With Jerry Lewis on *Jumping Jacks*. © Twentieth Century Fox.

With Mitzi Gaynor on *Bloodhounds on Broadway.* ©
Twentieth Century Fox.

With Debbie Reynolds on *Singing Nun.* © Metro-Goldwyn-Mayer Studios Inc.

With Cyd Charisse at the Dance In Action Awards in 1982.

With Harriet Parsons, Ann Francis and Louella Parsons on *Susan Slept Here.* © RKO Radio Pictures, Inc.

With June Allyson on *You Can't Run Away From It.* © 1955
Columbia Pictures Corp.

With June Allyson, Dick Powell and Jack Lemmon on location in Coronado, California for *You Can't Run Away From It.* © 1955 Columbia Pictures Corp.

With Sammy Cahn, Kirk Douglas and Burt Lancaster (reflected in mirror) rehearsing for the telecast of the Academy Awards. © 1956 Leonard McCombe

With Joan Collins and Rod Taylor on MGM Studios lot during filming of *The Opposite Sex.* © Bob Willoughby

With Ann-Margret and Jean Negulesco on location in Spain for *Pleasure Seekers*. © Twentieth Century Fox.

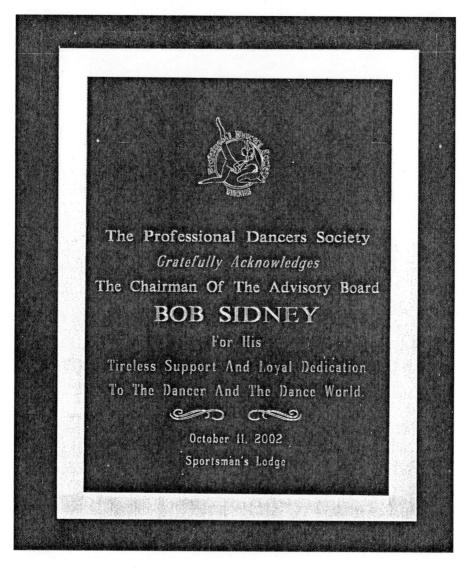

Professional Dancers Society Award, October 2002.

Irving Berlin Music Company

For: October 11, 2002

Professional Dancers Society
c/o Ms. Kate Kahn Williams
13112 Valleyheart Drive, #106
Studio City, CA 91604

To Members of the PDS,

We are so pleased that you are honoring Bob Sidney tonight at the
Professional Dancers Society gala. We recall the affection and
admiration that our father, Irving Berlin, felt for Bob Sidney and we
know he would join us in sending congratulations to Mr. Sidney and to
you all on this special occasion.

Sincerely,

Mary Ellin Barrett, Linda Emmet and Elizabeth Peters

Administrator: The R&H Organization
1065 Avenue of the Americas · Suite 2400 · New York, NY 10018 · Telephone: (212) 262-1800 · Fax: (212) 586-6155
Bert Fink, Vice President/Public Relations

Letter from Irving Berlin's daughters presented at the Professional
Dancers Society 2002 Fall Ball honoring Bob Sidney.

And More Stars...

Bing Crosby

Early in his career, Bing Crosby worked as a baggy pants comedian for Mack Sennett. He was no Charlie Chaplin or Buster Keaton, and never wanted to be. He only wanted to sing. He left Mack Sennett and teamed up with another beginner, Al Rinker, and they played little clubs as a piano singing act. Paul Whiteman was impressed with the duo, signed them, added another young singer, Harry Barris, and named the group The Rhythm Boys. It wasn't long before Bing's identifiable "Boo-Boo-Boo" caught on and almost immediately he became an important recording artist. Films followed, his celebrity grew and he was catapulted into the enviable group of living legends in the entertainment industry.

Much has been whispered about Bing's early life. He drank a great deal, caroused a lot, and was quite a ladies' man, even though he was married to Dixie Lee Crosby at the time. All that may be true, or much of it may be supposition, depending on the source. If one believes *Bing Crosby, The Hollow Man* by Don Sheppard and Bob Saltzer, an insinuating biography, then one should also believe the authors' admission that all the stories in the book were told to him by Dixie Lee herself. Don adds that if Dixie knew he published those stories, she would kill him. Doesn't it make sense to assume that Dixie Lee Crosby would never tell those stories to a biographer if she didn't want them printed? Here again, we have the biographer who writes sensational stories about people after they are dead and who no longer can defend themselves. I have a story Mr. Sheppard would not want to print. A dear friend of Dixie's, Kitty Good, who had once appeared in the Ziegfeld Follies and ended up the wardrobe mistress at The Nugget Nightclub in Reno, told Ray Arnett, who was Liberace's producer-director, that when Dixie would have one too many she would have a go at Bing. On one such occasion, Kitty accompanied Dixie to a showing at Don Loper's Salon and to spite Bing, who was very frugal, she ordered one of each gown in the collection.

Even though it would annoy Bing, I doubt that the biography, *Bing Crosby, The Hollow Man*, could keep him from losing sleep. However, Gary Crosby's autobiography, *Going My Own Way*, would definitely upset him. Gary's attempt at literary patricide was typical of the disgruntled offspring of prominent stars. Joan Crawford and Bette Davis also were targets for the poisoned darts of their daughters. In Gary's case, his own inadequacy tormented him and gave vent to an obsessive jealousy of Bing. Poor Gary. I suppose it is easier to be the father of a great man than to be his son.

My experience in the business has taught me to evaluate people as I find them. Other people's dislikes never influenced me. I am very grateful and proud to have worked with Bing. He was the consummate professional. You knew when he was pleased and when he liked you. Never a trace of emotion but his eyes telegraphed his feelings. He loved being around dancers. He knew where the laughs were.

When I first came to Hollywood, I was given a party in my honor by some of my gypsy friends who had worked with me on Broadway. A "gypsy" is an endearing term for a dancer, and it stuck because I imagine a dancer will travel anywhere where there is work. We were having a great reunion when the doorbell rang. It was Bing, who brought his own jug, as everyone else did, to the party. I was overwhelmed by how he blended in with the group. I suspected he had a crush on my friend, Audrey Westfall. You couldn't miss it, all you had to do was follow his eyes. It was an encouraging evening for me. After all, I was a stranger but I kept thinking if all the "stars" in Hollywood were as relaxed and casual as Bing, I would have no problem working in the film industry.

I never got to do a film with Bing, but I did get to do all of his Christmas Specials. Christmas is a time for the family and Bing was honest enough to parade his family on television. The first day of rehearsal was so unprofessionally professional. Bing arrived for the customary reading. He introduced his wife, Kathryn, who had been a contract actress, his son Harry, who loved music and could play a few instruments, his daughter Mary Frances, who wanted to be a ballerina, and his youngest, Nathaniel, who wanted no part of the entire proceedings and just wanted to be on the nearest golf course. Once these amenities were over, the Crosby family dug in and settled down to honest, no-nonsense work. They were a charming group. His kids mixed so well with everyone connected with the show. Rehearsals were a joy. Bing had one rule he wanted us to obey. He asked that we show his children no special favors. They were there to do a show and that was final.

That first Crosby Family show was so successful, it became an annual event. I was always amazed when the Crosby kids arrived for rehearsal after a year's hiatus. They seemed to grow so quickly. Harry played the guitar so much better; Mary Frances was sure of herself when doing her pirouettes; and Nathaniel still wanted to play golf. Only once was there a sign of temperament, and it came from Bing. We were doing a dance sequence in which the Crosby clan was dressed as hobos. It wasn't easy dancing in those heavy, exaggerated shoes. They had to do the number over and over again for the director to line up his shots. There were no complaints from any of the Crosbys. However, I did complain once they started to shoot the sequence. The director kept his camera on the street signs while the Crosbys were dancing and it finally settled on them for the last eight bars of the music. Bing was on my side and in a more than calm voice articulated, "We don't want to get in the way of your camera, so we'll be in our dressing rooms if and when you decide you'd like to shoot our number." That was the only time I saw "star" behavior on the part of Bing. After that incident he and I developed a very close relationship and he respected my opinion. More than once, he would ask me whether I approved of a certain line or whether he should sing a certain song.

I felt very special when Bing invited me to spend a week or two with the family in their home in Hillsborough, California. He was toying with the idea of doing an act with Kathy, Harry, Mary Frances and Nathaniel. The plan was for us to work on this project away from his agents and writers. I readily agreed because those characters often get in the way.

I arrived in San Francisco. Bing met me at the airport and we drove to Hillsborough. En route, I sensed Bing was upset, and indeed he was. He was troubled by his sons of his first marriage to Dixie Lee Crosby. The youngest, Lindsay, was into heavy drinking and popping pills, and was on his way to disaster. Gary, the oldest, was resentful and maladjusted. Dennis, one of the twins, had just disgraced himself in Las Vegas at a gaming table. He was drunk, grabbed the dice at a craps table, and, as he threw the dice, threw up all over the table. The other twin, Philip, was the only redeeming member of the group. He was definitely Bing's favorite. Bing thought Philip was a far better singer than Gary and he wished he would take singing seriously.

The Crosby home in Hillsborough, a very fashionable suburb of San Francisco, was very impressive. It housed a wonderful collection of paintings. My bedroom had some four or five beautiful works by Marie Laurencin. After I unpacked I met Bing in his study. He asked if I liked my room. I told him I did. He then asked if I liked the paintings in my room. I told him there was something very substantial about the prints. He broke up. I was happy my quip helped to restore his humor.

Bing and Kathy were very strict with their children, especially Kathy who on occasions reminded me of the traditional school marm. She hosted a daily talk show on radio. Before she would leave for the studio, she would wake Mary Frances. Kathy felt if she had to be up before dawn to get to her broadcast, then Mary Frances should be practicing her dance at that hour. "If one is to be in show business, then one should be ready to make sacrifices." It made no sense to me. Bing too had a problem with Mary Frances. He could understand adolescence in his boys but not in his daughter. He refused to accept that teenage girls developed breasts as they grew older. He objected to the V-shaped leotard she would be wearing in the show. He found it too revealing. He insisted she wear a turtleneck sweater. Of course, the sweater really exaggerated the outline of her chest. I finally convinced Bing that his daughter was now a young woman and fortunately had the healthy body a young woman should have. We had one more problem with the act. Bing hated to take bows; in fact, he didn't know how to take a proper bow. There are performers who increase the hand they get after a number by knowing how to bow. Bing didn't. I actually choreographed a series of bows, which he practiced as one would a dance step. But he said he felt like a "ham, milking the audience". The show played one night at San Jose College for some special benefit. It was well received and the young Crosbys turned in credible performances. Bing was pleased and that was important.

The act was shelved because Bing had a prior commitment to host a special, *Bing Crosby and Friends*. Bob Hope, Pearl Bailey and Bette Midler were to be guests on the show, which was to be filmed at the Ambassador College Auditorium in Pasadena, California. The run-through went very well. There were no technical problems and the performers were relaxed and enjoyed the informality of the show. However, the actual performance was a disaster. Bing was singing his medley unaware, as most of us were, that the back part of the stage was being lowered hydraulically to bring up a new set. No one informed us that this would happen, nor was it tried during the run through. It was one of those last minute "inspirations" on the part of some well-paid "genius" in the booth. Bing had just finished his set and as he was bowing he backed up and fell into the hole left by the lowered stage. We froze. No one breathed. Finally we rushed to Bing lying on the cement floor in the basement. Paramedics arrived. We were in a line as Bing was being wheeled out on a gurney. Pearl Bailey was standing next to me and was praying audibly. As Bing passed me I said, "Don't be late for rehearsal." Bing smiled and muttered, "You son of a bitch." We were ecstatic: he had finally spoken. He was alive.

That accident took its toll on Bing. He underwent heavy therapy but he bravely endured all the pain that was part of his rehabilitation because he was eager to start working again. He wrote and told me to prepare an act for Rosemary Clooney, the Joe Bushkin Quartet, his wife Kathy, his son Harry, and himself. We got an act together and we arrived in London, where we rehearsed on the legendary Palladium stage for about a week. One morning, while I was busy setting lights, Bing said if I didn't need him he would take a stroll. He needed fresh air. I warned him that his fans would mob him. He ignored me and he no sooner got some fifty feet from the theatre when he was surrounded by autograph seekers. It took a mounted policeman to disperse the crowds so that we could get him back to the theatre.

The billboards advertising our show went up in front of the Palladium and my name and credits were pointedly omitted. Bing collared his agent-manager and ordered that the error be corrected. When he was informed it was too late to do anything about it, Bing angrily announced, "Then in that case, the show is canceled." The correction was made.

Orchestra rehearsals went smoothly. Wonderful Rosemary Clooney was happy with the talented musicians; and Joe Bushkin, when he came down to earth, echoed her approval. Bing took little time to go over his music. He set tempos and that was it. He told the men in the band, "You just play and I'll sing along with you." I instructed the conductor to play Bing's theme song, *When the Blue of the Day* on his entrance. Bing insisted there was no need for that. He would walk on cold when he was introduced. I alerted the conductor to be prepared for at least sixteen bars of music to cover Bing's entrance. On opening night the orchestra had to play the entire song over twice and the audience was still applauding and cheering. I was convinced Bing didn't believe his own celebrity. The show was an enormous hit. Bing was elated. That mattered to me.

After the London engagement, his agent hoped Bing would accept an on-going offer to play in Japan, where he would be a sell-out. Bing resisted vehemently. He never forgave Pearl Harbor. The success of the show and the confidence that the show would be a hit anywhere influenced his change of heart. He told me that if we played Japan, the show would be mine. He didn't need the money nor could he afford to take it, what with taxes and all the rest that goes with being rich. He insisted the whole show was my creation and that it justly belonged to me. He only asked that I boost Rosemary Clooney's salary. This whole proposition was mind-boggling to me. I was overwhelmed. I had to blink and shake myself before it set in. No one had ever been that kind and appreciative. All this from Bing Crosby, whom many had called cold and insensitive.

Closing night in London, I had a strange premonition. Something prompted me to ask Bing for his autograph. I don't know why. I had never asked anyone for an autograph before. I decided I would get everyone else's signature first before I approached Bing, otherwise he would think I was joking. When I got to Rosemary Clooney, she asked if I sensed something too. We didn't expound on our feelings but we were both on the same wavelength. As I suspected, Bing laughed when I asked him to sign the program I was carrying. I showed him that all the others had signed and I convinced him I honestly wanted his autograph. He was very pensive and finally wrote, "With eternal gratitude – Bing". I have that program in a very handsome silver frame. It is one of the most cherished mementos I own.

After a brilliant run in London, we were obliged contractually to do a one-nighter in Brighton. The stage was a series of platforms, the sound was bad and there were few lamps to work with, but the audience was so appreciative, Bing gave his all. They made him sing encore after encore. Finally, it was over. Bing was in high spirits. He was leaving for a holiday in Spain, where he was to play golf on one of the best courses in Europe. Bing died while playing golf. Perhaps he would have liked it that way. But I believe Bing Crosby would have preferred meeting his Lord with a microphone in his hand.

<u>Rita Hayworth</u>

Rita Hayworth, the celluloid goddess, the fantasy of most males between puberty and senility, the Columbia Pictures superstar, the vixen with the challenging smile. She was all of that and more on the screen, but in real life Rita Hayworth was insecure and timid.

In the film *Loves of Carmen*, Rita was to do a dance with one of the male gypsies. I was assigned to choreograph and rehearse the number with Rita alone before the actual shooting began on the picture. Then at a later date, when they were close to filming the sequence, they would engage Rita's partner and I would have three days to teach him his part, after which Rita would have two days to work with him. Panic set in when production informed us they were ready to shoot the dance sequence sometime during the next two days. Both Rita and I tried to explain to Charlie Vidor, the director, that there was no way anyone who didn't know the number could just jump in and do it. Vidor said "Let Bob do it, he should know his own number". Rita agreed and the next morning there I was dressed and made up to look like a gypsy, albeit an unwilling one. On the way to the set, Rita kept telling me not to worry, I would do great. When we arrived at the stage, Rita froze. She was terrified of the crowd of extras who were there to dress the set. She was actually trembling until someone shouted, "Roll 'em", and suddenly as if another soul had taken over her body, her energy and total abandonment were electrifying. She was now the other Rita. She was in command; she was secure with her lover, the camera.

Working with Rita was a treat. She was disciplined, determined, yet great fun. She could relax and forget being a "star". She was warm, considerate and grateful for the smallest of favors. We had a strong rapport. We became friends.

After Rita's marriage to Orson Welles ended, she went on holiday to France where she met Prince Aly Khan. The meeting wasn't a casual one. It was orchestrated by Elsa Maxwell, the party-giver, and in this case, the matchmaker. Aly was smitten by Rita and very soon afterward they were married. Rita found herself in world of mystery, a strangely different culture, a society that played games that could destroy the unsuspecting, and living a life that was constrained by the responsibility and decorum that went with the title Princess Margarita Aly Khan.

I was on a tour of Europe and one of my friends asked me to accompany him to Gstaad. Off we went. We no sooner checked into the Palace Hotel when my friend casually mentioned that Rita and Aly had a chalet very close to the hotel. "Wouldn't it be great fun to drop in on Rita". I forgot to mention my friend was an American. I was coaxed into sending a note to Rita. I simply wrote I heard she was in Gstaad, and if it were convenient, I would love to say hello, and if it weren't I would understand; after all she was now a Princess who might choose to forget Hollywood. The phone rang. It was Rita. She insisted I come right over, bring your friend, you can unpack later. Rita behaved like a child who had found her favorite lost toy. Aly was not at the chalet. He was in hospital nursing his wounds after a bad spill on the slopes. Rita introduced us to a most likeable woman, Princess Andree, the third wife of the Aga, and with the greatest of pomp and delight Rita presented her infant baby, Yasmine. Other than sleeping at the hotel, we spent all our time with Rita, Princess Andree and Aly Khan. The night before we left for Paris, we gave a "thank you" dinner party. Rita asked if she could bring Aly's son, Karim, who is now the present Aga Khan. Of course! We escorted our guest to the dining room at the hotel. Both the concierge and maitre d' were relieved and reassured when they saw Rita and Princess Andree with us. They explained that the entire staff at the hotel thought my friend and I were two American gangsters on the lam. Before leaving, Rita gave me the number at *L'Horizon*, their home just outside of Cannes, and I in turn gave her my address in Paris. A week or so later, Aly, Rita and family returned to *L'Horizon*.

We soon met up again. I was in Cap D'Antibes and phoned Rita. Once again she insisted I come right over. She had to entertain some special guests for lunch the next day and needed help. Aly had invited the Duke of Alba, the admiral of the U.S. 6th Fleet and his wife, a reporter from *Paris Match*, a horse breeder from Ireland, and an art dealer from London. It was a strange mixture of guests and Aly opportunely suffered a relapse and asked me to take his place. Poor Rita, she had to cope with French, Spanish, English and the persistent admiral's wife, who had had one wine too many and kept inviting all of us to a party on board the flagship of the 6th Fleet. She even asked Rita to bring the old Aga along. When Rita politely explained that the Aga couldn't possibly manage the gangplank, Mrs. 6th Fleet said, "No problem, we'll hoist him up in one of those nets they use for loading cargo." The afternoon was a nightmare, yet Rita bravely saw it through. Aly loved to have guests around but he was too busy to entertain them. That became Rita's responsibility. He also enjoyed attending all of the galas that were so popular during the season in the south of France. Rita didn't. They were too much like a movie premiere, with the photographers, the press and the autograph hounds. Aly relished showing off Rita to his friends, as he would one of his prize thoroughbreds. Rita resented the comparison; it was beginning to challenge her patience.

When the Aga Khan went to India for the jubilee celebrating his birthday, Rita and Yasmine were brought along. They were very important to the spectacle. Rita, who was still a popular movie star, and Yasmine, who had the distinction of being the first female descendant of Fatima in two hundred years, were the special attractions of the event. In the past the Aga's weight was measured in gold, whereas this time it was precious jewels. Rita could manage the chanting of thousands of worshipers but she cringed when some of the faithful bathed and kissed the feet of the royal party of which she was one.

In Cannes, Rita was asked to present the cup to the winners of a pro-am golf tournament. The newspaper announced the event and almost immediately afterward, Rita received a note from the Aga hastily written on ordinary scrap paper. It said that the Aga was not pleased that she chose to embarrass him and his family by making a public spectacle of herself. He hoped she wasn't that desperate for publicity. Rita defiantly wrote back and told the Aga that the only reason she agreed to present the award, was that the chairman of the tournament was sure the Aga and his pro golfing partner would win the match and the charity affair would have special significance if she made the presentation. As for publicity, she reminded the Aga she had enough of that in America and in the rest of the world before she ever came to Cannes. It was the Begum, the Aga's wife, who incited the Aga's anger. She bitterly resented Rita because no one ever mentioned her in the press since Rita arrived in Cannes. The frightful woman thought she was a match for Rita because she once won a beauty contest. She used every ruse she could muster to distance Rita from the Aga, and she succeeded. Rita paid back in kind when she was pushed too far by the Begum. Rita's background, half Spanish and half English, gave her the fire and the calm she needed in those crises.

The rift between Rita and the Aga and his Begum grew into a family feud. Aly remained neutral, even though he shared Rita's dislike for the Begum. He depended entirely upon his father for his vast allowance and to oppose the Begum would incur the displeasure of his father. That situation added to the pressures weighing on Rita's reserve.

Aly was an inveterate gambler. He squandered his money and some of Rita's too. But the most difficult thing for Rita to endure were the rumors in some society salons that Aly was having an affair with a very popular model. Unfortunately, they were true. Rita had made up her mind. She was leaving – but how to take the little Princess Yasmine with her? She knew the Aga and Aly would forbid it. She had the perfect excuse. Harry Cohn, her old boss at Columbia Pictures, threatened to sue if she didn't return to Hollywood to finish out her contract. She owed the studio one more picture for which he would double her salary. It worked and Rita, Yasmine and Rebecca, her daughter by Orson Welles, arrived in New York. I had a message at my place; a Mrs. Brown at the Plaza Hotel had called me. I phoned the Plaza and was delighted to learn Mrs. Brown was our Rita. We decided to celebrate her return at the Versailles Room, where the incomparable Edith Piaf was to open that night. As we entered the club, newsboys were yelling, "Cerdan killed in a plane crash". Cerdan was France's foremost prize-fighter and Piaf's favorite lover. We were sure she couldn't possibly go on that night, when we heard a drum roll followed by the simple announcement, "Edith Piaf". There she was, "the little sparrow", in her customary black dress. We admired her courage: she showed not the slightest awareness of her personal tragedy until she sang *La Vie En Rose*, the love poem she had written for Cerdan. Rita sobbed unashamedly. I wondered if it were for Piaf and Cerdan or for herself and Aly.

Rita's return to Hollywood wasn't heralded as the event of the year. Other than the speculation concerning the status of her marriage, which she glossed over gracefully, people were genuinely civil and concerned for her privacy. Harry Cohn did have a film assignment for her. She was to play the other woman in the catastrophic film version of Broadway's *Pal Joey*, starring Kim Novak. She silently endured Harry Cohn's cruelty in holding her to her contract but giving her a supporting instead of a leading role. Her problem was not the studio, or the rented house, or the responsibilities of looking after Yasmine and Rebecca. Her problem was within herself, the struggle between the present Rita Hayworth and the former Princess Margarita Aly Khan. Was she happier now than then? It was rumored that Rita was drinking heavily and that she was always drunk. True, she couldn't take a sip of wine without seeming drunk. Yet she drank far more wine in Paris without reeling. The truth is that no one knew too much about Alzheimer's then. It didn't seem likely that a woman as young as Rita could possibly have that mysterious illness. And besides, it was far easier to condemn than understand. Her daughter Yasmine did understand and took Rita back with her from Los Angeles to New York, where she was cared for as one would expect a Celluloid Goddess should be.

I can never forgive the female biographer who in her sleazy account of Rita Hayworth's life story blatantly accuses Rita and her father of having an incestuous affair. She claims the source for that information was Orson Welles, who was married to Rita. Of course, Orson Welles is dead, so I ask you, the reader, is it conceivable that a woman having sex with her husband in bed cries out, "My father did it better than you!"

June Allyson

June Allyson's career started the very day she saw her first movie. Her grandmother took her to the local movie house where little June, who was about five years old at the time, was mesmerized by the images she saw on the screen. She wanted to reach out and touch them. She wanted to he near them. She knew she too belonged up there on that screen. It has always been so for June Allyson. Her romance with movies is undeniably a very happy lifetime relationship.

Junie, as her friends always refer to her, spent hours watching movies. They became her teachers. She learned to dance watching Fred Astaire and Ginger Rogers before she ever took a lesson. In fact, she saw *Gay Divorcee* at least twelve times. She was a dedicated observer and a very talented pupil. When Junie was still in high school, her friends goaded her and urged her to audition for a Broadway show. She did and was picked for *Very Warm for May*. Several other musicals followed – she was now a true gypsy. She understudied Betty Hutton in *Panama Hattie* and went on for her several times, always stopping the show, which led to one of the leads in *Best Foot Forward*, a George Abbott musical. And in true Hollywood tradition she was signed by MGM, where her auspicious career mushroomed after proving her talent wasn't limited only to musicals such as *Good News*, *Till the Clouds Roll By* and *Words and Music*, but that she could easily handle dramatic roles such as *The Stratton Story*, *Little Women* and *The Glenn Miller Story*.

In the movie industry, the truly outstanding performers become superstars, because of their talent or unique quality of personality that sets them apart. Greta Garbo, Bette Davis, Betty Grable and Katharine Hepburn are prime examples of such artists. June Allyson certainly occupies a place on this list. She was voted the number one artist at the box office in 1955, and was the number one female box office attraction in the country for six consecutive years. Junie even found time to have her own show on television, *The DuPont Show*. She is a true star who never works at acting like one. Junie is one of the most relaxed artists to work with and that infectious smile of hers is as sincere as she is.

Junie was never one of the Beverly Hills denizens. She likes having her friends around her, whether they are actors or stagehands. Junie and her husband, Dick Powell, used to entertain close friends at their estate in Mandeville Canyon. I remember one night we were there for a barbecue with Doris Day and her husband, Marty Melcher. Junie sang a song, Dick sang a song, and then Doris sang a song. And another song. And another song. Finally, Marty turned to Doris and said, "You've turned down Las Vegas nightclub acts, yet you've practically done an act tonight. You could have made us a fortune." Prophetically, he lost her a fortune. He mismanaged her finances and owed her a reported $20 million.

Junie has been accused of being overly friendly with her leading men. In fact, Alan Ladd's wife, Sue Carroll, made a point of that in her book. Actually, there's no truth to those stories. Because Junie, fortunately or unfortunately (unfortunately, I guess) is the sort of person who is always kissing people. She has to do that. It doesn't matter who the person is. I think sometimes people mistake that for intimacy. I've been with her on several films and I have never seen her do anything that would be questionable.

One thing Junie has always been guilty of is that she gives too much of herself to her friends. As a matter of fact, when we were doing *The Opposite Sex*, one of Junie's co-stars Carolyn Jones told me that her very talented husband unfortunately was having trouble finding a job as a writer. She asked me to talk to Junie and ask her husband Dick Powell, who was then the President of Four Star Television, to arrange an interview. Junie did, and Dick signed Carolyn's husband as a writer and producer. That man's name was Aaron Spelling, who later became a very important man in television. Aaron and Carolyn were later divorced, and when Carolyn needed help, Aaron was not there for her. Nor was he there at her funeral, which Junie arranged herself. She flew down from Ojai, where she is living with her present husband, Dr. Ashrow.

June Allyson is a very human person. I appreciate her sincerity, even though there were many people in Hollywood who, for some curious reason, have either been jealous of her girl-next-door image or tried to destroy that image because she is too wholesome. Junie is wholesome and I prefer her that way.

Liberace

I never thought I would choose to see a Liberace show, but I did and only because I had to. A very close friend Ray Arnett had just been signed on as producer/director of the Liberace show and he asked if I could be there, if only to make suggestions, so I showed up at the Pan Pacific. The show was out of doors and the sun scorching hot, which made me a very unhappy, non-receptive audience for any performer. The show began predictably. Liberace made his entrance wearing sequins and furs. Then he sat down and played the piano. But as I watched the show gradually I realized I was being cued when to laugh and when to applaud. It occurred to me that Liberace onstage was manipulating the audience, as well as myself. He was a masterful puppeteer and we were his puppets. I was very impressed. I was so interested in watching his technique that I suddenly realized that this man was a craftsman, a brilliant craftsman. At the end of the show I unashamedly joined the others in giving him a well-earned standing ovation. I cheered as loudly as they did.

After that show, I became a Liberace fan. I got to know him well enough to call him "Lee", a name reserved for friends only. I was present at many Christmases in Las Vegas when he would give lavish parties. I also would be at his home on certain occasions when he would give a big dinner party with his dear mother Frances, whom he adored. And she liked me. Consequently, I became one of the family as far as she was concerned. At a dinner party, before dinner was served, she'd say to me, "Get in there. Be ready. Because when the door opens all these vultures will be in there and there'll be nothing left for you to eat." Frances was something. One night at Liberace's show in Las Vegas, I was sitting next to her at ringside. Suddenly, as Liberace was performing, she whispered to me, "Help me put my fur coat on." She had this huge mink coat draped all over the chair and I helped her put it on just as Lee said, "Ladies and Gentlemen, my mother." And on cue Frances stood up, dripping with mink. The audience applauded and Liberace ad-libbed, "Ma, you're wearing one of my coats again."

Early in his career, Liberace played most of the good clubs. His act at the time was very proper, he played piano and he played beautifully and that was it. One day on his way to work, he passed an antique shop and he saw something in the window that attracted him. He bought it and took it with him to the club. He didn't want to leave it in his dressing room because he was afraid someone would run off with it. So he brought it onstage and put it on the piano. It was the candelabra that later became one of his trademarks. That candelabra led to a gold lamé jacket, which in turn led to a sequined jacket. All that outrageous extravaganza brought him much attention, which led to his own television show. On the air, he was a favorite especially with the purple-haired ladies who loved him as though he was their own son. Liberace appealed to the younger people and sometimes they would laugh at him, but he would beat you to the punch because he'd be laughing at himself. As he would say onstage, "Go on, have fun. You're paying for it, you may as well enjoy it!"

Liberace had a persistent mania for buying and then redecorating homes. My favorite of all was his home in Palm Springs. It had a chapel connected to it. Not that Liberace was religious, but it made for a conversation piece. In the main house his bathroom was huge. The sunken marble tub, above which hung a beautiful baccarat chandelier, was almost the size of a small swimming pool. The ceiling in his bedroom was a replica of Michelangelo's Sistine Chapel in the Vatican in Rome. The subject matter was the delightful little cherubs, one of which had Liberace's face painted on it. When he was lying in bed he could look up and there he was looking down at himself. Liberace wasn't very social – he was too preoccupied with his nightclub act, which he was constantly changing, always adding something outrageously exotic, which his public expected of him. And he gave them more than they asked for. He would make his entrance in a Rolls Royce, the body of which was entirely covered by little mirrors. His wardrobe was really costumes designed by Michael Travis. It was very theatrical and very expensive. He wore a white fox cape and the lining was all rhinestones. Reportedly it cost over $150,000. Lee's theory was: "The more you spend the more you earn." In his case that formula worked beautifully.

His finale really was impressive. He'd start to play serious music, usually Chopin, and suddenly these dancing waters would become a live background and the stage he was sitting on would revolve. It was really a sight to see and quite tasteful and always got a big standing ovation. Liberace once decided, after he saw *Mary Poppins*, that it would be fun if he could fly at the end of a show. So he was rigged in the flying gear and he was told not to flail his arms, otherwise he might turn over. As Lee ascended, he started waving and blowing kisses at the audience. Just what he was told not to do. The waving and kiss blowing made him flip around and around, and finally the gear got caught in the grid (the place where they keep the lights way above) and there was Liberace, hanging, glued to the ceiling as it were. All they could do was lower the curtain. Liberace couldn't see the standing ovation he received.

Liberace was scheduled to appear on *The Dean Martin Show*. I was very excited because I would finally get to work with Lee. But our producer, as most producers usually have strange ideas, did not want Liberace to play the piano. However, I worked around it and when I saw Lee I told him exactly the situation. He wasn't temperamental at all. Another performer would have said, "I'm not going to appear, nobody's going to tell me what to do." But Lee just said, "Let's do something about it." So I asked if he knew any dance music. He said, "I know the *Beer Barrel Polka*." I said, "Great. Here's what we'll do. You and the orchestra will start playing the polka. One of the dancing girls will come out, get you away from the piano and start dancing with you, and the orchestra will take over. You get back to your piano again, and just as you do another girl dancer will come out and get you just as the first one did. This happens repeatedly until all the six girls get you up and you dance with all of them. At the very end you are so exhausted, you collapse at the piano and the girls all drape around you." The number went very well. Liberace got his usual ovation. And I could breathe normally again.

Of all of Lee's creations his favorite was The Liberace Museum in Las Vegas. The museum housed all of his memorabilia, some of his very ornate wardrobe, a few of his Rolls Royces, the valuable antiques he collected, letters and citations from important personages, and a photographic history tracing the early Liberace up to the present. The museum was and still is one of the favorite tourist attractions in Las Vegas. The money the museum makes does not go to Liberace's personal estate. It goes to a foundation Lee established in his will. The foundation gives scholarships and grants to needy and talented young musicians whom the trustees hope will reach the level of the artistry of the serious Liberace – the performer who was on his way to becoming a very important concert pianist, that is, before he was sidetracked by his sequins.

Sonja Henie

Sonja Henie, the darling doll-like "Norwegian Queen of the Ice", was the bitch of all times. One need only study that frozen smile and those piercing steel-blue eyes and suddenly her face dissolves into one of the terrifying horrors in the traditional Volsunga Saga.

In all fairness to Sonja, her career and her achievements have never been equalled by any other skater. She was the holder of three Olympic and ten World Championships, not forgetting the countless trophies, medals and special awards she had earned. Most importantly, she more than any one else was responsible for making the skating business a multi-million dollar industry. One would hope with all that going on for her she would at least have feigned humility. Not Sonja! Her philosophy was hard and blunt. One wins, no matter what it takes, or else one fails in life. The glory and prestige of just being a contender who tries their best in an Olympic event was meaningless to her. It had no honor. I think a medal and an orgasm were both the same for Sonja.

I am not a skater; in fact I have never worn a pair of skates. It was the very talented Catherine Littlefield, who had done most of the Henie Ice Shows, who decided, for some flattering reason, to be my mentor and help shape my career. She insisted I stage the upcoming ice show. It didn't matter to Catherine that I couldn't skate; yet she managed to sell me to Sonja as someone who would bring a freshness to her show. A meeting was arranged at the very chic Colony in New York. I arrived in time and was seated by the *maitre d'* just as Sonja made her entrance. And what an entrance! She was busier than a humming bird in heat. She was accompanied by a dear, frightened woman whom she called "Mor", Norwegian for Mom. As she sat in the booth, she casually threw a litter of furs she had been wearing onto the floor and announced, "They're sable, you know". Right there and then I should have left and double-timed it to the nearest taxi, yet I remained glued to my seat, astonished by the spectacle being performed for my benefit. I thought it only fair to tell her I knew nothing about skating and when I did, she said not to worry, she would guide me. In fact, she didn't talk about the ice show but she went on about the ice she was wearing. You couldn't see her arms for all the gems she had on – and at lunch time too. Cartier on wheels!

Rehearsals were held in a huge enclosed arena in San Bernardino, California. It was agreed I would have two days alone with the skaters. I was very concerned that first day because I had never worked with skaters. In fact, I had never even met one. I was delighted to find them very co-operative and friendly. I had never heard about "inner" and "outer" edges and how they limited what a pair of skates could do, and the very first combination I designed violated the basic principle of those damned edges. Even though those valiant souls thought it wouldn't work, they gave their all and to their – and surely my – amazement things began to happen. Of course adjustments had to be made but the combination was different and they were excited, as something new had been added to their world. My new friends realized there was more to life than one and one makes two. I was in!

Skaters are their own people. They're not dancers, they're not athletes, they're the magical link in between. It cannot be denied that Peggy Fleming has the grace and elegance of a prima ballerina, and Dorothy Hammel has the endurance and exerts as much energy as the world record holder Jackie Joyner Kersee. What would Mikhail Baryshnikov give to be able to match Brian Boitano when he handily executes a triple-axel leap in the air? It's gratifying to know that skaters have finally arrived. An ice show special on prime time television is sure of high ratings and makes for excellent family viewing.

Back to Sonja. She arrived, as scheduled, on the third day of rehearsals. She didn't say hello but casually mentioned she had been told I was planning to undermine the rules of skating. It didn't take long for me to discover she had her own awkward system of espionage, namely three pathetic stooges who ran over each other trying to prove their devotion. Sonja and I clashed almost immediately, and when she loudly announced she had made a serious mistake in hiring an amateur, I agreed with her and insisted she fire me, which of course was the last thing she wanted to do. Not that she was concerned about having to pay off my ten-week guarantee, which incidentally I would have gladly forfeited. No, she wanted me around so that she would have someone official to blame if something went wrong. If she failed to execute a proper turn on the ice, she would rant she was under undue pressure and when I told her to straighten her knee when performing an aerial, which is what is termed an arabesque in the ballet world, she was apoplectic. No one dared say she wasn't the perfect skater. Actually, she was when it came to school figures. Those are compulsory in competition and they represent an important percentage in evaluating the ability of the contestant. Sonja could score a circle on the ice and then skate over that circle four or five times and never deviate from the original scoring one eighth of an inch. Unfortunately, one cannot see that part of the competition unless one is standing alongside the skater. In freestyle skating, Sonja wasn't breathtakingly graceful and she had average *tour de force* which wouldn't do today. Kristi Yamaguchi could leap a triple-axel to Sonja's badly executed one-and-a-half. When Sonja performed the cross-foot spin, the trick most skaters use at the end of a number when they turn so rapidly they look like a blur, her shoulders were hunched and her head was buried in her neck, whereas when most skaters do the same trick, it's done with grace and almost perfect posture.

The show finally opened in San Francisco at the Cow Palace. In spite of Sonja's constant prediction of disaster, the reviews were glowing. I would have loved to have witnessed her reaction when she read those. Unfortunately, I'll never know because my contract ended on opening night. I said goodbye to my skater friends and even waved goodbye to Sonja. It was exhilarating to be free again and breathe the dung of the Cow Palace.

To really know and understand Sonja Henie, one would have to study the stories attributed to her. Some are as incredible as she was herself. When Sonja was a teenager, she represented Norway in the Olympics held in England. The skaters were assigned to an area adjacent to the curling rink. Curling is a sport very much like our bowling, except that it is played on ice. Special attendants brush and guard that ice with religious fervor. It is sacred land to the curler. Sonja resented working out with the other skaters near her, so she took her skates over to the curling rink and before the attendants could get to her, she had ruined the ice with her sudden stops, leaps and spins. It became an international scandal, important enough to be brought to the attention of the Royal Court in Norway. The Norwegian ambassador met with Sonja, tried to reprimand her, demanded an apology to which Sonja replied, and this is a quote from the culprit herself, "I told him to inform the King that if he wanted me to win a gold medal to let me do it my way without his help". All this from a teenager!

Sonja was signed by Twentieth Century Fox and became one of their biggest grossers. The studio paid heavily for that. She drove every department mental. She would tell the lighting director what lamps to use; the cinematographer couldn't line up a shot unless she approved it; and she even dared tell her fellow actors how to read their lines. They would start shooting a very expensive skating sequence with Sonja wearing an elaborate head-dress, which she chose herself, and after two days of filming she would testily decide she didn't want to wear the head-dress, which meant they had to re-shoot the number from the beginning. The studio rejoiced when her contract ended and many parties were given to celebrate her departure.

Sonja had a reputation for being a very shrewd businesswoman. That wasn't the case. It was her brother, Leif, who invested her money wisely in real estate and made her millions. He was devoted to her, yet she cut him out of her will. She didn't like his wife.

Sonja was once detained by French customs as she entered Paris. They politely asked her several times if she had forgotten to declare some diamonds she had bought in Amsterdam. She was outraged. How dare anyone question her honesty. Unfortunately for her the customs people had been alerted about the gems by the dealer in Amsterdam, who would receive a good share of the penalty if she were guilty. Sonja was obliged to submit to a search. She was led to a dressing room where she was examined by a huge police woman. Sonja gave her two one hundred-dollar bills which the police lady gratefully accepted and then couldn't wait to tell the custom agents that Sonja indeed had the diamonds concealed on her person. Sonja was betrayed. She savagely attacked the woman, ripped off her blouse and triumphantly retrieved the two hundred dollar bills from the bosom of the terrified lady agent. It took several gendarmes to subdue Sonja. I asked her if she wasn't embarrassed by the scene and she said "Are you crazy? It made great publicity."

Sonja decided she needed a social background to go with her persona as an international star. She found a property in Norway with great potential and it was converted into an impressive manor house.

She stocked it with important antiques and romantic paintings. She even sat for a portrait of herself that graced the entrance hall of the mansion. Sonja then unashamedly boasted that all this splendor had belonged to her family for generations. To strengthen that image, she annexed a husband, the American socialite Winthrop Gardner, who truly had the proper background. His was a very old social family. Early during rehearsals of the show, where we worked Monday through Friday and then had the weekend off, her husband arrived on a Thursday, obviously to surprise Sonja. When she saw him, she grabbed the microphone out of my hand and shouted, "What are you doing here, I only need you on the weekend". The poor man, instant bloodless emasculation!

Sonja is now immortalized in her personal Valhalla, The Sonja Henie Museum, formerly her "family home" in Norway, where the visitor can pay homage to "the darling doll-like Queen of the Ice" and study her portrait "with that frozen smile and those piercing steel-blue eyes", and wonder!

Milton Berle

If the Magna Carta had some jokes in it, Milton Berle would insist he wrote it. The self-appointed, self-anointed king of comedy wore his crown successfully for some 65 years. There have been contenders to challenge him, but he adroitly handled the competition. He would graciously admit that the newcomer had great talent and add, "Why shouldn't he? I taught him everything he knows and he's using my material. And besides, how can he miss?" Milton felt that he has an inborn right to anything that's funny. That was his domain and it belonged to no one else.

Milton's career started when he was a young kid. He was a member of the *Gus Edwards Kiddie Review*. They were just a line of young boys and girls – dancers and singers – who were very popular at the time. Milton's mother Sondra, who guided his career, didn't think too much of the chances for advancement in that situation. She thought he couldn't go too far as a member of the song and dance group. So one night she asked him, "When you people make your entrance on stage, what foot do you come out on?" Milton said, "We enter on our left foot." She said, "Well tonight you will enter on your right foot." That night he did and the result was predictable. Milton tripped some of the kids, they fell on him and the audience howled with laughter. When the show was over, instead of shouting and yelling at Milton, the producer said, "Tomorrow night you do the very same thing." Milton did, and with each performance the laughter got louder and louder. Milton realized what they were laughing at and he would play up to it.

He didn't realize it, but he was now a comedian. He liked the sound of laughter more than the sound of applause. Every true comedian loves the sound of laughter. It's a philosophy that followed Milton to vaudeville and nightclubs. In fact, he broke all attendance records at the Carnival Room at the Capital Hotel on Eighth Avenue with his nightclub act. The room was open ostensibly for a four week run with Milton. He stayed there for months and months. People came from uptown, downtown, East Side, West Side. He was the biggest comedy attraction Broadway had ever seen.

His comedy wasn't cruel or vicious, nor was it topical or political. His comedy was direct, not subtle. He wanted people to laugh immediately. He went in for baggy pants, blacked-out teeth, toupees, funny costumes and quite often dressed in drag. People accused him of enjoying drag far too much. He didn't deny it. He said he loved getting in drag, except that he couldn't manage the high heels.

About that time, a new medium had captured the imagination of the American public – television. Milton Berle exploded on the screen his first time out. He was a phenomenon. People tuned in not to NBC, but to see Uncle Miltie. He was a joy and he also could be a terror to work with. I remember once he asked me to do a comic ballet piece for *A Streetcar Named Desire*. I did and when I showed it to him there were people standing by – electricians, some visitors – and it got a few laughs. Before I finished, Milton was up running for the stage, hopped up ready to perform. Sondra, his mother, said to me, "Milton will get more laughs than you did, I promise you." I said to Sondra, "If I got his salary I'd get more laughs too."

In any case, Milton was up there enjoying every bit of it. He improvised and added bits and pieces to what I showed him. Milton could improvise brilliantly. He was a very quick study. All you had to do was show him something once, and he could repeat it immediately. On the same show, we had a great opera star, Helen Traubel. The dear lady was singing her aria during rehearsal, when Milton jumped up on stage again and said, "You're not holding the note long enough. And you're not breathing right!" He was telling the lady how to sing. You almost felt he wanted to sing the aria for her. Fortunately, the lady had a good sense of humor and went along with it because it was getting a lot of laughs.

Milton remembered that bit, and when he had a guest that didn't have a great talent, he would have them sing a song and he would repeat with this guest what he did with Madame Traubel. Or he would compound it. He would take far more liberties than he would dare with her. He would open the singer's mouth. He would look down his throat for other notes. He would reach in the singer's trousers to straighten his shirt. He did all sorts of ridiculous nonsense that got laughs. And that's all that Milton wanted.

But his intrusions didn't stop there. He would tell the lighting people how to light the show. He would tell the conductor how to conduct the music. He would even grab the baton and show him what he meant. He would tell the costume designer what was wrong with the costumes. Milton had to get into everybody's way, literally. He meant well, but he really made you work hard for your money. There were times you wanted to leave but you couldn't possibly, because you knew he was just reaching for laughs and we understood his wishes. He needed people around him who had a sense of humor. Some of us did.

Earlier, I had told Milton that I was leaving for the Coast to do a film I was committed to. On the night I was to leave, I came to say goodbye. He wouldn't hear of it. He ignored me completely. I stood in the wings. I wanted to be polite. So when the curtain came down I rushed out and said, "Goodbye, Milton, I'm leaving." He grabbed me, he held me, he hugged me, he kissed me. And the curtain came up for his bow and there the audience saw two men in an embrace. Well, they were laughing. They didn't know what to make of it. It was funny. The curtain came down again. I started to move and he said, "Don't move. We're getting laughs. Stay where you are. We're getting laughs, don't you understand? Laughs." Curtain went up – then he had me in a backbend. Curtain came down. It came up again – he held me in another fancy position. It looked as though we were about to do a tango. Somehow, I managed to pull away from him and I was on my way to the Coast.

I last saw Milton at the Friar's Club where he looked very frail and weak. His wife Lorna and an attendant helped him shuffle to his table. Once there, he slouched and almost fell into his seat. He slumped over and he was panting heavily in that position, when the Master of Ceremonies announced "Ladies and Gentlemen, tonight we have the one and only Milton Berle." And as if by magic, his body stiffened, he sat up erect, and then somehow he got to his feet. He stood tall. Taller than his peers around him who were giving him a standing ovation. The applause was deafening. And Milton had the most sublime smile on his face. I will always remember Milton Berle as he was that night.

Bob Hope

Bob Hope was to the movies what Milton Berle was to television. These two ambassadors made comedy, but were very different in their styles. Whereas Milton was a hard-punching, obvious comedian who got laughs and got them fast, Bob Hope is more sophisticated. His manner is very casual, very offhand. If a joke didn't work, it didn't matter. He did one-liners all the time and always had another one in readiness because he had a very talented staff who supplied him with excellent material. The jokes worked everywhere. In the Pacific, where he entertained our troops, or in Washington, where he amused some of the big politicians, Hope was triumphant with the one-liner.

But he really gained great prominence when he started to work with Bing Crosby and Dorothy Lamour at Paramount Studios. The Publicity Department at Paramount built up this imaginary feud between Bing and Bob and that caught on with the public, although they knew it wasn't quite true. However, in truth, there was a little rivalry. I remember once when I was doing a Christmas special with Bing Crosby, he said to me, "What do you make of this Bob Hope? Has he gone crazy? Look at him. He's over 80 and he's still chasing girls." Bob Hope, on the other hand, said to me once, "You did that special for Bing. Did you have a lot of pretty chorines there? Because Bing goes for that you know in a big way." Actually, the big contest between the two was who was richer, Bing or Bob. It's reported that during his career Bing sold hundreds of millions of records and his worth, based on that, would be hundreds of millions of dollars. Whereas Bob Hope, we all know, owns most of North Hollywood in the Valley. His properties there are important and located in strategic commercial areas. And so he has a tremendous amount of wealth. And so one will never know which one is richer, because each accused the other of being very, very rich. In any case, we don't have to worry about either man, they've had the wherewithal to enjoy life to the fullest.

Bob Hope, like many important performers, did not like to share his prominence with others. I remember once I did a revival of Roberta, a musical in which Bob Hope made his reputation on Broadway. The revival was a condensed version and was to be played at Southern

Methodist University. I imagine that Bob knew some of the big oil people down there and they talked him into doing the performance. In any event, the show we did wasn't quite the script that was done on Broadway. It was just a vehicle for Bob Hope. In the show, we had Janis Page, and Bob asked me to do a show-stopping number for her. I staged a song and dance number for her and two boys that actually did stop the show. It was based on a Fred Astaire number called *I Won't Dance*. The applause was quite thunderous when Bob Hope, who was ready to go on next, came rushing out of his dressing room. He said, "What's going on? What's happening?" I said, "Janis just stopped the show." He said, "What do you mean?" I said, "She stopped the show. You said you wanted a show stopping number." He said, "You didn't have to listen to me, did you?" as he gaily skipped on the stage in that frivolous manner of his.

Bob Hope has been known to be a prankster on several occasions. Once, at a gala performance in England for a worthwhile charity, some of America's outstanding performers were contributing their talent. Bob was standing next to Jack Benny. Jack was amusing some of the other American performers, who were on edge because they had been told they were going to be presented to Her Majesty, the Queen of England. Jack went on about how there was no reason to be nervous, that Her Majesty was just another human being like everyone else, and that we were Americans, so we didn't have to pay total homage to her. It would be sufficiently polite to bow our heads a little bit and not as the British do, since they were her subjects. As he was going on about what to do, what was protocol, what was polite and proper, the Queen was about to approach where Bob and Jack were standing. Bob leaned over to Jack and whispered "Your fly is open," just as Her Majesty reached Jack. Jack bent so far over, trying to cover what might need to be covered, I'm sure the Queen must have thought that this American bows lower than any of her subjects. Bob Hope was a prankster.

On an Academy Awards® Show which I co-produced with Joseph Pasternak, we were excited when we were told that Bob Hope was going to be the Master of Ceremonies, because there were very few people who qualify and can handle that position as well as Bob Hope. The day of the show was a long one – rehearsals that lasted forever. The show was to go on at about 8 o'clock. It was about a quarter of 8, and Bob told Joe and me, "I'm going into my dressing room. I'm going to lie down for a few minutes." And we said, "You can't lie down, the show goes on in 20 minutes." He said, "I promise you I'll be fine. Just have someone call me at 10 minutes of 8." Of course we had someone standing guard at that door, and at the appointed time we knocked on Bob Hope's door. He came out very casually, removed the Kleenex that kept the makeup from staining his collar, put his jacket on, and walked blithely to the stage just as they announced "Here he is, our Master of Ceremonies, Bob Hope." He came on stage in a casual manner. Both Joe and I were amazed at this powerhouse who was out there ad-libbing and being funny as usual. There's no doubt in my mind that the title "Mr. Show Business" really does apply to Bob Hope.

Bob Hope's trophy room in his home is a treasure trove of priceless personal memorabilia. The walls are lined with autographed photos of him with the world's famous people. Among those are world leaders such as: Juan Carlos I, the former king of Spain; President Franklin Delano Roosevelt and all Presidents who succeeded him, up to and including Richard Nixon; Winston Churchill; Charles de Gaulle; important statesmen such as Chamberlain and Kissinger; and even winners of the golf tournament that bears his name. Strewn about the room are trophies that Bob was given by organizations in gratitude for his help to them. He also has citations from the Unites States Armed Forces for all the time he spent in the Pacific entertaining our troops and lifting their morale.

In a special display is his most important award – the Congressional Gold Medal, given to a citizen for outstanding service to the country. Bob deserved it. I venture that Bob Hope and Irving Berlin were two citizens who did more for the morale of our military personnel than any politician who might have been elected. It would be wonderful someday if Bob's trophy room was moved intact to the Library of Congress in Washington, D.C., because thousands of tourists visit that museum daily. That way, Bob could always have an audience.

Tallulah Bankhead

Tallulah Bankhead has been called immoral, degenerate, promiscuous, unreliable, patriotic, a true Southern Belle, an affected Southern Bitch, and many more questionable appellations. She would fiercely object to being identified with any single one of these characterizations, yet she would proudly admit to being all of them together at the same time. La Bankhead was outrageously amoral. Conventional behavior was good for the soul but bad for the digestion. Long before Tallulah was identified with Regina, the predatory character she played in *The Little Foxes*, she displayed a will astonishing in someone so young.

When Tallulah was about twelve, her daddy cautioned her that some of his fellow congressmen were coming to the house for an early toddy. He begged her to be on her best behavior and added, "Honey, I don't mind you smoking when the gentlemen are here but please no cussing." To his astonishment she never smoked once but she swore non-stop, words even her daddy never used when he was in a fury. Congressman Bankhead learned his lesson. From that day on, if he wanted his "dahlin' Tallu" to do something, he would ask her not to.

Tallulah was destined for the theatre. She had the flare, the daring. She was a true exhibitionist. She no sooner made her mark on Broadway, when off she went to London where she was critically acclaimed for her performance in *Rain*, the play in which Jeanne Eagles starred on Broadway. Tallu was instantly accepted by the London theatre crowd. She was the featured guest on everyone's party list, as well as the very private playmate of a promising young officer in the Home Office. Unfortunately her lover would share state secrets with her, if only to impress her with his importance. One night she accompanied him to an important political gathering where Winston Churchill and other important statesmen were in a heated discussion concerning the U.S. refusal to join the League of Nations, even though it was conceived by President Woodrow Wilson. They were being very patronizing about America's position on foreign affairs, when Tallulah took over. No one, not even Churchill and company, could denigrate her country. She was playing a role. It didn't matter whether her arguments had any merit. She was center stage and she had what she thought was a captive audience. How dare they criticize the United States when their planned campaign in India would violate the basic laws of the League of Nations? Unwittingly, she repeated everything her lover had told her in the privacy of her bedroom. The young statesman was banished to one of the farthest British colonies and Tallulah was asked to leave England immediately. Estelle Winwood, the very popular English theatre star, interceded on Tallulah's behalf and Miss Bankhead was permitted to remain just long enough to settle her affairs before being booted out of the country. Her comment concerning this scandal was typical and unrelated: "The English are dreadful lovers, they yawn during orgasm."

Tallulah loved to be on the attack. She was known to go at people for no earthly reason. Jimmy Gardiner, who produced the last *Ziegfeld Follies* in which she starred, once asked her why she disliked Bette Davis so vehemently. She indignantly replied, "Dislike her? Dahling, I don't even know her. Here's a woman who can't sing, she can't dance, she can't walk, she can't act, and yet she's a big movie star. Dislike her? On the contrary I admire the cunt." Another of her victims was Gertrude Lawrence. Miss Lawrence never did anything to offend Tallu, but it didn't matter – Tallulah had an unrelenting dislike for her. On opening night of *Susan and God*, the first act curtain had just come down when Tallulah rushed backstage past the bewildered doorman and was about to knock on Gertie Lawrence's dressing room door when the stage manager intercepted her in time. She insisted she came backstage because she had to tell Gertie how marvelous she was in the play. The confused stage manager reminded her this was only the first act; and he suggested she come back after the show and then congratulate Miss Lawrence. To which Tallulah offered, "After the show, are you mad! By that time she will have fucked up the whole thing."

Tallulah loved to play bridge and her constant partner was her inseparable friend, Estelle Winwood, who was as fey as Tallulah was unpredictable. Dear Estelle invariably overbid her hand and as a consequence a disgruntled Tallulah was always the "dummy". On this one occasion when Estelle was wildly bidding small slams and a few six no trumps, Tallulah was angrily bored. She went to the phone and called her husband, John Emery, in Hollywood. She didn't bother to say hello. She simply said, "I'm divorcing you John", and then hung up. When she was asked what was all that about, she said, "I had to do something, I just can't sit here and be the "dummy" all night."

I was asked to stage a number for the Navy Relief Ball at Madison Square Garden. Tallulah was one of the celebrities in it and since she insisted she had never done musical comedy before, she demanded she be given special rehearsal time. I arrived at her hotel, the Elysee, after being warned she would probably receive me while she was sitting on the "john", as she usually did just to shock people. I arrived on time, rang the bell and heard that throaty voice order "Come in, the door's open". She wasn't on the "john" as I expected, but she was in her tub, stark naked. She feigned modesty when she saw me and covered her breasts. She then stood up in the tub, raised her left knee and, using it as a pointer, indicated a towel on a rack and most politely asked me to hand it to her.

During the Second World War, Tallu was stylishly patriotic. She even vowed she'd never take a drink until the war was over. No one ever saw her break that vow but she sure could get high just thinking about a martini. Now and then she would call the U.S.O. and have them invite wounded servicemen to her home in New Bedford. On one such occasion, she phoned some of her card-playing cronies, Vivienne Segal, star of *Pal Joey*, Eleanor Holm, former Olympic swimmer and wife of the producer Billy Rose, and her favorite bridge partner, Estelle Winwood. Tallu cautioned Vivienne and Eleanor to please try hard to behave and refrain from vulgarity. Estelle needed no admonition; she didn't approve of profanity. Vivienne and Eleanor arrived dressed for the part. They wore picture hats and little white gloves, and entertained the soldiers by the swimming pool. Their behavior was impeccable. Vivienne asked one of the boys where he was from. Of course she knew his city so well, she appeared there several times. Eleanor told the boys that swimming was great therapy to help restore the use of injured muscles. Before Estelle could say something typically whimsical, Tallulah announced, "Viv, see the taller one with cast on his leg? He tried to fuck me last night." Vivienne and Eleanor were stunned, and Estelle, hoping to ease the tension, chirped, "Which reminds me, some of my "gay" friends took me to a "drag" in Harlem last week, and everyone wanted to dance with me, they thought I was in "drag" too." With that Vivienne, who couldn't swim, fell into the pool and she would have drowned if Eleanor hadn't been there to save her.

Tallulah didn't approve of sentimentality and I have reason to believe she was afraid of it. On her bedside table there was a triptych with three photographs of one of the most beautiful, captivating faces I had ever seen. When I asked Tallulah who this young woman was, she became very quiet and finally sighed, "She was my mother. She died in childbirth when I was born. I never knew Mama, but I know she's always with me." She turned her head away, hoping I wouldn't see her tears. It was very reassuring to know that Tallulah Bankhead could also be human!

Ray Bolger

Ray Bolger could do more in a skirt than Sylvester Stallone ever could in his boxing shorts. Ray loved dressing in drag, albeit he wasn't as outrageous or blatant as Milton Berle had always been. Bolger was more sensitive and legitimate. And legitimate he was, every six nights and two matinees on Broadway in *Where's Charlie*. Ray loved playing Charlie's aunt. It was his favorite role because he could shamelessly romp all over the stage in his dress. Even though it was dowdy and Victorian in style, it was far more glamorous than the costume he wore as The Straw Man in *The Wizard of Oz*. Disregarding whatever his preference may have been, it was *The Wizard of Oz* that gave him the reputation he enjoyed as a singing and dancing comedian. That was actually a far stretch because Ray did not sing well and his dancing was star quality when it was eccentric. His dance vocabulary wasn't too extensive. He excelled in doing steps that bordered on the awkward and the precipitous. You laughed when he was off balance and most often he was when he seriously tried to do a pirouette.

Bolger started his career as a ballroom dancer. He got laughs when he shouldn't have and as a result he could never hold on to a partner. Ray met his wife Gwen when she was one of the acts at the club where he and his partner of the moment were performing. Gwen sang and played piano. She was far ahead of the times and just like Ray she was getting nowhere, even though she had a very interesting sound and wrote good music. When Ray's partner left him because she was too humiliated by the laughs their serious routines were getting, Gwen moved in. They hardly knew each other when they were married, with Gwen vowing to be his manager "till death us do part". She recognized Ray's potential as a dancing comedian and she was determined he would make it big. He had to. If she was willing to give up her career, which has to be the most painful sacrifice an aspiring artist can make, then Ray had better attain the goal she set for him. She was determined he would be one of the best in the business. His success would be her reward.

Gwen labored to have him booked into more tony nightclubs than he had played in the past and even succeeded in getting him to headline on the better vaudeville circuits. He finally landed on Broadway and from then on it was up and up to the top. Gwen never allowed him to take a serious role. Comedy would be his *forté*. If his singing wasn't the best, it didn't matter. Comedians could even get laughs trying to sing. Only once did Gwen relent, when she allowed Ray to dance seriously in the George Balanchine Ballet *Slaughter on Tenth Avenue* in the musical *On Your Toes*. The audience started to snicker through some of the serious parts of the ballet. Ray was smart and quick enough to fall back on his sure-fire steps that always got laughs. He turned what was almost a tragedy into the greatest success he had had up to that time. His career was secured and he joined the ranks of the stellar performers, thanks to Gwen's guidance and "show biz savvy".

The Bolgers rarely frequented haunts like Sardi's, where theatre people lunched after matinees or supped after the evening show. They were more likely to be seen on the East Side with the upper class. Fortunately for Ray, none of his cast was present when he affected the broad A or he would have been sure to get some of the biggest laughs he ever got. In spite of Gwen's ambition for him, Ray retained a healthy amount of modesty. Unlike his peers, he never talked about when he stopped the show or his meteoric rise to stardom, and only, I suspect, because he didn't believe it himself.

Vivienne Segal

Ethel Merman was the number one leading musical comedy star on Broadway but Vivienne Segal ran a close second. The ladies had one thing in common: they *started* their careers as stars. Neither ever struggled to get to the top. Ethel Merman stepped on a stage, never having been on one in her life, in *Girl Crazy*, sang *I Got Rhythm* and became an overnight sensation. Vivienne Segal, in a similar manner, sang *Auf Wiedersehn* in *The Blue Paradise* the first time she ever stepped on a stage.

The Vivienne Segal story is enchanting, because it sounds more like a fairy tale, or at least a scenario for an old-fashioned Warner Brothers musical comedy. The Shubert brothers, the legendary producers on Broadway, were trying out *The Blue Paradise*, one of their operettas, in Philadelphia. They were having trouble with the show, rewrites and music changes. To stimulate interest at the box office, they conducted a contest where they promised the winner a small part in the show.

Vivienne, at the age of 17, had already established herself locally in church concerts as a very young singer with talent. She won the contest easily. Her mother, Paula, who was a frustrated actress, told the Shuberts that rather than giving her daughter a small part in the show, she would like Vivienne to be allowed to attend all the rehearsals so she could learn about the business.

Vivienne never missed a rehearsal, even though she missed school. The leading man in the show, J. Harold Murray, was enchanted by this young girl and her beautiful voice. During lunch breaks he would sing the duets with her. He would even coach her in singing the leading lady's numbers. Finally, the show went to New York and left Vivienne in Philadelphia. In New York City, three days before *The Blue Paradise* opened, the leading lady was stricken with appendicitis and was rushed to hospital for immediate surgery.

The Shuberts were beside themselves. That meant closing the show. The leading man insisted that they call for this young girl in Philadelphia. She knew the role, he told them. He had gone over it many times with her and she'd be wonderful. But they would not hear of it. Finally, he told them, "What have we got to lose? We close the show or we try this girl?"

Vivienne was sent for and after one day's rehearsal, she stepped on stage on Broadway and became an immediate star. She was the find of the Great White Way, the darling of Broadway. So much so that a very prestigious nightclub, The New Amsterdam Roof on top of the New Amsterdam Theater on 42nd Street, invited her to appear there – a great honor. They instructed her to get her act ready and to have one encore, because that was what all the performers there usually got.

Vivienne opened, and just as they promised, she did her act and was called back to do an encore. She was ready to leave the stage, but they wouldn't let her go. They kept applauding for more and more and she said, "I don't have any more songs to sing. However, my accompanist has written some wonderful little tunes he has taught me. We sang them in rehearsal, so with your permission, may I sing one or two for you?" Of course the audience cheered and when she finished she said, "Now, ladies and gentlemen, I would like you to meet my accompanist...George Gershwin."

Vivienne next worked for the great impresario Florenz Ziegfeld. She starred in all of his operettas and even ended up starring in his *Ziegfeld Follies* along with Fanny Brice, Will Rogers and Bert Williams. Fanny and Vivienne became great friends. One of Ziegfeld's most important backers, a railroad magnet, was giving a party for his friends. Ziegfeld asked Vivienne, Fanny and some of the show girls if they would go. It was a polite affair, nothing with nude girls flying about. It was just a lot of rich men with pretty girls around them. Vivienne and Fanny were seated at dinner, when Fanny asked Vivienne if she would go to the powder room with her.

They excused themselves and when they got there, Fanny said, "Did you see what each girl got under her plate?" Vivienne said she didn't notice. "Each girl got a hundred dollar bill, and we got nothing. So let's get the hell out of here." Vivienne said, "No, no, no. That would be bad manners. Let's go back, eat their dinner, then get the hell out of here."

Vivienne finally ended up in Hollywood, where she really didn't belong. The film medium was not for her, but she did get to meet old friends who had now become prominent Hollywood citizens. One day at a party, someone asked her, "Did you hear Carole Lombard? She says the filthiest things." Vivienne answered, "I know, dear – I taught her those."

Vivienne returned to Broadway and worked for Ziegfeld again, but unfortunately she fell in love with the stage actor Bill Boyd, who was a scion of a rich family. He had a drinking problem and Vivienne became addicted to drink herself. At the ripe age of 30, she disappeared from the theater. When Bill Boyd died, Vivienne had to get her act together and had to struggle to be acknowledged again in the theater.

Fortunately, at Jones Beach, outside of New York City, there was a big outdoor show during the summer, usually operettas. Vivienne, having sung in each one of those shows previously, was hired. She became a fixture. People came out to hear her and enjoy her performance.

It rained almost every other night at Jones Beach, and it was difficult for the poor performers on stage. They had to continue to perform, no matter what. Larry Hart, of the song-writing team Rodgers and Hart, was there one night during a terrible rainstorm. People wouldn't leave, and finally Vivienne walked to the footlights and pleaded, "Why don't you bastards go home?"

Larry was delighted. He loved it, and he reported to Dick Rodgers immediately, saying, "You know Vivienne Segal could play the chic, wry countess in *I Married an Angel*." Dick agreed, and they sent for Vivienne. Vivienne went to the theater, thinking it was a reading of the play. But when she got there, the stage manager said, "You're on third." She said that she didn't understand. He said, "You're at an audition, Miss Segal."

She bit her lip and waited. When her name was called, she came out and Dick Rodgers very condescendingly said, "We want to know if you can still sing. Do you have a song you can sing for us?" She said, "I don't have any music with me, but I know the national anthem." So she sang *The Star Spangled Banner* beautifully. When it was over, Dick said, "Vivienne, you didn't have to do all of that." And she said, "That's quite all right, Dick. You know, I've never had to audition in my life, and you made that possible today. I shall never forget that." Vivienne played in *I Married an Angel* and was very successful. Broadway acclaimed her as a "great comedienne."

I joined the show when it went on tour. I was in the Ballanchine ballet, and I was also understudy to Burl Ives, who was at least three times as large as I was. On this tour, we had our own company train, which put us in very close quarters. Perhaps too close in some instances. Especially when Burl Ives, who was drinking heavily on the tour, would sing his ballads endlessly, keeping all of us up at night. We heard *Jimmy Crack Corn* so many times, we urged him to shut up and told him where to shove Jimmy Crack Corn. Little did we know it would become his biggest hit as a balladeer.

Also, living in close quarters made us privy to all the current gossip. We knew who was sleeping with whom and when. I remember one of the singing ladies was having an affair with one of the singing men in the show. The problem was that he was married, but not to her. As we got closer to Los Angeles, he warned her that his wife would be waiting there for him and they would have to put their romance on hold. But she was very dramatic about the whole affair, complaining and crying to anyone who would listen. When she told her sad story to Vivienne, Vivienne said, "You must remember, he's a married man. You must respect that." And the girl protested, "but Vivienne, you don't understand. I'm in love with him. He's torn my heart apart." To which Vivienne replied, "What a strange place for your heart to be."

When we got to California, Burl went on a drunk. On opening day, our poor stage manager went mad when he was apprised of Burl's condition. They sent for me immediately, and they tried to get me into his uniform. He played the part of General Lucash.

I swam in the outfit. They tried to pin it together as much as they could, and they put zinc oxide to gray my hair. On stage in the opening scene, I was supposed to tell everybody about a big surprise party we were giving. I was naturally very nervous. I felt like an idiot, dressed the way I was.

It had been announced that an understudy was going on that night, and usually in that situation the audience is very sympathetic. When Vivienne made her entrance, to put me at ease, instead of saying her usual opening line, "Oh General, it's a delight to see you again," she said, "My God, General Lucash, you've lost weight, haven't you?" Of course I broke up, the cast broke up and so did the audience. From that day on, it was easy sailing. They did fix the suit to fit me, but I played Burl Ives' part for the rest of the run with that damn zinc oxide in my hair. Vivienne and I became very close friends, a friendship that lasted forever.

I staged and choreographed one of Vivienne's shows, the ill-fated *Toplitski of Notre Dame*. It was actually a precursor of *Damn Yankees*, with a very similar story. Instead of a fantasy about baseball, it had Satan and a football hero. Critics were not kind to the book, saying, "the plot was preposterous." Yet they loved that plot when *Damn Yankees* came around. But the dances got raves. Burns Mantle of the *New York Daily News* called it "the best dancing on Broadway." Unfortunately, *Toplitski* only lasted a few weeks.

When Vivienne did *Pal Joey*, which was probably her greatest triumph, she got every award – the Critics Award, the Donaldson Award. She was now established as a deft comedienne. During the Dress Parade (the occasion when all members of the cast wear their costumes and parade in front of the director, the choreographer and the producer), Vivienne refused to put on the gown that was designed for her. She had warned the costume designer that she would not consider the dress, saying it was not the sort of thing she would ever wear. Vivienne did have great style. Finally, when she was called, she arrived on stage with her mink coat on.

Now George Abbott, the director, would faint if a woman ever said "damn." He was very proper. He said to her, "Why wouldn't you put on that gown?" She shot back, "Because horseshit looks better on me, George." Abbott passed out. He had to be revived.

Dick Rodgers' social-climbing wife Dorothy made it clear that she did not want Vivienne at the opening night party they were giving. She told Larry Hart that Vivienne's profanity would shake up the whole affair, since there were important society people coming. Somebody pointed out to Dorothy that she couldn't give a cast party without the star. Vivienne was finally invited.

But Larry had something of the devil in him, and told Vivienne that Dorothy really didn't want her there. However, Vivienne arrived at the party, dressed very chicly, and was perfectly charming with everyone. She enchanted her audience. When it was time to leave, Dorothy walked her to the door and told her, "Vivienne, you can't imagine how happy you've made me, coming here. You were the hit of the party. It would have been nothing without you." "But you must admit, Dorothy," Vivienne answered, in a voice that echoed throughout the room, "I didn't say 'son-of-a-bitch' or 'fuck' once." And so, with that, she repaid Dick Rodgers for the audition he put her through, and exited.

Vivienne went on to play one or two other shows and finally married Hubbell Robinson, the Executive Vice President of CBS. She accepted that role in her life. She enjoyed being the hostess, entertaining very important guests she knew personally. Finally, after Hubbell died, Vivienne retired in Beverly Hills, where she lived modestly in a very attractive little house.

Unfortunately, she was victimized by a corrupt servant. The Los Angeles County Probate Court did nothing to remedy the situation, and Vivienne died without any of her friends at her bedside. Vivienne Segal didn't have an audience at the end. It would have made her very unhappy if she had known that.

The Andrews Sisters

The Andrews Sisters, Patty, Maxine and Laverne, in that status order, were indisputably the foremost singing group of the '40s and '50s, and I dare say there have been very few groups to equal their sound and harmony since. They were monumental stars on record, radio, television and film. Patty was the ringleader, the captain, the bully. Her word was law; when she cracked the whip, the other two fell in line. Maxine was the hit-man who got the dirty work done. She even married her agent so that she could control their bookings and contracts. And dear, sweet Laverne never made waves. She remained in the background, embarrassed too easily to voice her opinion, which would be ignored in any case.

Fresh out of the army, I got the job directing a *Colgate Hour Special* starring Tony Martin. The Andrews Sisters were one of the important guests. Our booking agent was so excited to have them on the show, he overlooked one clause they insisted upon in their contract, namely they were to have a ten-minute spot for their medley. The show was 30-minutes long, with eight minutes allotted to commercials. That left only 22 minutes for the entire production. After deducting the ten minutes for the Andrews spot, Tony Martin, who was the star, was left with twelve minutes for himself and the other performers. The Andrews Sisters wouldn't budge, they were to have their ten-minute spot or they would "walk" and then sue the show for breach of contract. As director of the show I called a meeting with the girls and their agent. Reason could not prevail. Even though all this happened early in my career, I had been around long enough to smell "ham", which could be traced to Patty. I guessed, rightly, she was a frustrated leading lady and I wasn't going to let my acting classes at school go to waste, so I improvised a very touching scene about the show being ruined because there wouldn't be time for two strong spots, namely the love song and the funny sketch for the comedian. Patty wasn't moved at all. Just when I realized my acting classes were a waste of time, Patty added, "I don't give a damn about the love song, I don't get to sing it". Without thinking, I blurted out, "But you do. It's a duet for you and Tony Martin." I got carried away and added, "You also play the woman in the comedy sketch." It worked. Patty went for the bait. She demurely asked how long would these two sequences take and I innocently whispered, "About six minutes". I was ecstatic when Patty volunteered, "We have a four minute medley which probably would be better for the show than the eight minute one". I thought all was lost when Maxine started to object but before she could voice her objections, Patty silenced her with a look.

Patty did get to sing the love song with Tony Martin. However, it was hardly romantic, it was more comedic. We dressed Tony in a little Lord Fauntelroy suit and Patty in a pinafore with the largest bow on her derriere. We used an oversized set and oversized props, which gave the illusion that they were small children in an ice cream parlor. The love duet went out the window; each one was too busy topping the other. But it worked, the audience roared at this fresh version of a love song. Patty's sketch with the comedian was a variation of the court room scene so popular in burlesque shows. She played the gal with the free-swinging hips whose dialogue is punctuated with bumps and grinds. She loved playing the part and got so carried away she added bumps and grinds where they weren't needed. She was getting laughs. To hell with the medley, she was now a comedienne who sang. The show went very well, but I had nightmares that night. I kept thinking what if it hadn't!

Debbie Reynolds

When Debbie was quite young, her two recurring fantasies were a peanut butter sandwich and a bed of her own, an army cot she wouldn't have to share with her grandfather. Our national depression had conquered many a family but not the Reynolds clan. They were proud, resourceful and determined. Her dad had heard that Southern California was the land of opportunity, so they went west in search of a better life, leaving El Paso behind them. Mr. Reynolds was quite happy to quit his job working for the railroad. They paid so badly; it was almost impossible to support his brood.

The Reynolds' caravan finally made it to California. They avoided "sinful" Hollywood because they were members of the Nazarene faith, which prohibited any activity other than reading the Bible, so the family settled in heavenly Burbank.

Mary Frances, which was Debbie's real name, adjusted quickly to her new environment. She was so impressed and amazed at the many activities her new school had to offer, she couldn't decide on which one to choose, so she joined them all. She auditioned for the marching band and was chosen to play the French horn because she was the only one who could balance that heavy instrument and march in step at the same time. She was very popular and was voted the girl most likely to succeed. Her chums adored Mary Frances so much, they couldn't do enough for her. They even entered her in The Miss Burbank Beauty Pageant, which she won. A Warner Brothers talent scout was at the pageant and was so taken with Mary Frances, he arranged a screen test for her.

The studio heads decided the girl had a great potential and they signed her to a starlet's contract, after first changing her name to Debbie. Her contract paid very little, hardly enough to buy a simple outfit. Since Debbie's mother, Maxine, sewed all of her daughter's clothes, the Reynolds' budget was way ahead.

Warner Brothers didn't know how to use Debbie, so when her contract expired, she was let go. Fortunately, MGM borrowed her test.

They were so impressed, she was signed to join their family of contract players.

Once at MGM, Debbie was mesmerized by this huge citadel of entertainment, with its stable of her favorite stars, its well-organized school to teach and train the newcomers, and an incredible publicity department that plastered your name and photograph all over town even before you had turned one foot of film. This studio did know how to use Debbie. She was groomed carefully. She was given minor roles at first and she even got to sing and record *Aba Daba Honeymoon*, which became a huge hit and rated high on the music charts.

About this time, I was signed by RKO to stage and choreograph the numbers in *Susan Slept Here* starring Robert Mitchum and introducing the newcomer Debbie Reynolds. Because of a prior commitment, Mitchum dropped out and was replaced by Dick Powell, who was the producer/director of the film.

At my first meeting with Miss Reynolds my instinct warned me that this loveable brat would take over if I let her. So right then and there I established my position, which she never challenged. We became instant friends and we still are. Fortunately, Debbie was very fond of my assistant, Ellen Ray, who gave her *ballet barre* each morning before rehearsals began. During breaks, Debbie regaled us with stories about the young, macho actors who dated her and, because she rejected their crude advances, had decided Debbie had to be gay, else how could she resist them. That sort of vicious rumor does get around. Debbie wasn't bothered one bit, in fact she laughed at the notion. There is a lesson to learn here: never try to deny or dispel a rumor, on the contrary, encourage it and it will fade away. As I said, in *Susan Slept Here* there is a dream sequence in which Debbie imagines she's a little canary in a gilded cage. We rehearsed the number in a huge mock-up of the little cage, which through the magic of special effects could be reduced in size to look like a little cage, with Debbie on the perch swinging back and forth, doing tricks on the bar. Of course, we had a double for Debbie. Although the poor double never got to do any part of the routine, since Debbie insisted on doing all of it herself, even the dangerous fall off the perch when the cage was dropped some forty feet. *Susan Slept Here* got great reviews and Miss Reynolds returned to MGM a star.

Someplace, somewhere, somehow Debbie met Eddie Fisher and they were married. The press made much of this idyllic union. Soon after, Carrie and Todd were born, and Debbie loved being a mother and housewife. Unfortunately, Eddie was always away on the road working. Unfortunately, too, Eddie's flagrant affairs with other women were no secret and when Debbie actually discovered his infidelity, the romance hit a sour note and they got divorced.

Curiously, Debbie never allowed anyone to bad mouth Eddie when her children, Carrie and Todd, were around. They were led to believe that their daddy, Eddie, was very, very busy and he would see them when and where he could. I remember one Christmas Eve at Debbie's where Rudy Render, her vocal coach, and I were both wrapping gifts for Carrie and Todd and signing the cards from Daddy Eddie. Debbie wanted it that way.

Debbie was married three times and struck out three times. After Eddie, she married Harry Karl, the shoe merchant. They had a good relationship that was based on respect. However, Harry was an inveterate gambler who lost his money as well as Debbie's at the craps table, the races, card games, or at any sporting event. Their marriage ended amicably.

Her third husband, Richard Hamlet, was a total surprise to all of her closest friends. He didn't belong. His only association with her world, the theatre, was his surname, Hamlet. My take on that marriage is that Debbie, who wasn't too knowledgeable about Shakespeare, believed that by marrying Hamlet she was making her contribution to culture.

I worked with Debbie on *How the West Was Won*. Some of the locations in the mountains of Colorado were the most difficult ever. We were snowbound by Winter storms. Debbie had to shoot scenes in the freezing rivers wearing clothes more appropriate for Spring. Yet she never complained.

My happiest association with Debbie was when I wrote and staged her highly successful Las Vegas nightclub act. We designed the act to prove to the executives at MGM that she would be perfect for the lead in *The Unsinkable Molly Brown*, over the objections of the director Charles Walters. Opening night at the Riviera Hotel was a triumph for Debbie.

The audience stood and cheered and wouldn't let her off the stage. Both Debbie and I knew then that the part was hers and deservedly so. She was brilliant in the film too.

Her debut in the nightclub business gave her the assurance that she could work in any medium. She excelled on Broadway in a revival of the musical *Irene*. She's a frequent guest on television and she has even tackled the lecture tour circuit. Debbie has been and is still involved in civic affairs. Almost single-handedly, she started the Thalians, a very important organization dedicated to helping emotionally disturbed children. They are now an affiliate of Cedars Sinai Hospital. True, her hotel in Las Vegas failed, but only because the gambling commission wouldn't grant her a license, without which a hotel cannot exist in Las Vegas, no matter how good the show is – and Debbie's show was good. She even appealed to the Governor and explained that over the years her show had brought many tourists to Las Vegas and that she had also been a resident of that city since her first appearance there. Yet she was turned down. It's strange, but if she had been a gangster's moll she would have had no problem getting a license. Knowing Debbie Reynolds, I'm sure she would and could have played the part of a gangster's moll gladly, if it would have helped.

Cyd Charisse

Cyd Charisse was born Tula Ellice Finklea in Amarillo, Texas. When her older brother was three, he couldn't say her name "Tula" and so tried to call her "sister" or "sis". He tried and tried but was unable to and finally came up with "Sid" for "sis". From then on she was called "Sid" by everyone during most of her teens.

When Sid was twelve, she was far too thin. She was always tired and had little energy. The Finklea family doctor prescribed exercise for her, lots of it. Her father thought that the best way for a young girl to exercise was to dance, so he enrolled his daughter in the local ballet school. After a few months of classes, Sid put on weight; regained her energy and, more importantly, developed a love for dancing.

After Sid's second year at the ballet school, her teacher told the Finkleas that their daughter was wasting her time in Amarillo; she should be studying in Los Angeles, where there were excellent schools for advanced students. Sid's father organized a trip to visit some old friends in Los Angeles and while there he hoped to find the right school for Sid. We are all familiar with the idea of the predatory "stage mother" – well Sid's father was fast taking on that role.

Once in Los Angeles, Sid began her studies at the prestigious Adolph Bolm Ballet School. Maestro Bolm was very impressed with his new pupil, so much so that he gave her private lessons. One eventful afternoon during class, Colonel de Basil of the Ballet Russe de Monte Carlo came to see his old friend Adolph Bolm. The Colonel immediately noticed Sid and announced that this beautiful young dancer had to join his company. Of course Mr. Finklea agreed but he stipulated that his young daughter was to be the Colonel's direct responsibility.

Now that Sid was to be a member of a Russian ballet company, she needed to have a Russian name. The Colonel christened her Maria Istomina, without the Texas accent, of course. And now Tula, or was it Sid, or was it Maria, well, one of them, joined the American tour of the Ballet Russe de Monte Carlo.

The night before the company was to sail for Europe, Sid was told that her father was seriously ill. She flew home to Texas to be with him, and the Ballet Russe de Monte Carlo left without Maria Istomina. Her father never regained his health and after his death, she rejoined the ballet company in France. Colonel de Basil assigned a young married couple to be her guardians, famed choreographer-dancer David Lichine and his wife, Tania Riabouchinska, one of the prima ballerinas in the company. The Colonel decided that he didn't like her stage name and changed it once again. She was now called Felia Siderova and to this day she never quite knew why. In spite of her two chaperones, the company ballet master, Nico Charisse, courted this young dancer and married her. In time, they had a son, Nicky, who is now a respected lawyer in Northern California. Because of the War, our State Department urged all Americans to return home. Sid returned to California and her mother came to live with her and look after Nicky, if and when Sid got to work again. Fortunately, she did. MGM was looking for a young, beautiful ballerina to be featured in *Ziegfeld Follies*. The studio found and settled on Sid. After viewing the first day's rushes Bob Alton, at that time the dean of all musical choreographers, was so excited he insisted that Arthur Freed, the producer of *Ziegfeld Follies*, sign the girl to a long contract. However, the contract was held up because Arthur Freed objected to her name, which he said was a boy's name. Sid argued that since she had been given so many names in the past, she would like to be called by the name she grew up with. Finally, Arthur Freed suggested "Cyd", which after all was pronounced "Sid", the only difference being the spelling. So she was now Cyd – Cyd Charisse – a dancer in *Ziegfeld Follies*. Coincidentally, Tony Martin was starring in *Ziegfeld Follies*, yet he and Cyd never got to work together in the film, nor even meet at that time.

The word was out. The longest and most beautiful legs in Hollywood belonged to the young ballerina MGM had signed – Cyd Charisse. Almost immediately, every eligible bachelor and playboy went on the prowl. Cyd kept them at a distance. However, two persistent admirers finally made contact with her. One was the enigmatic billionaire oilman Howard Hughes; the other was the singing star Tony Martin. Howard Hughes used his usual approach, showering Cyd with limousines, flowers and gifts. But that got him nowhere. However, Cyd was impressed when Howard Hughes taught her how to fly a plane. On the other hand, Tony Martin's approach was more romantic. He escorted Cyd to wonderful parties and I suspect serenaded her with songs. Howard Hughes was aware of the competition, but also knew that Tony was a playboy and couldn't possibly be serious about Cyd. In order to get rid of him, he gave Tony two tickets on Hughes' airline TWA to take Tony and one of his lady friends anywhere they wanted to go. Tony accepted this kind offer and used the tickets for himself and his new bride – Cyd Charisse. It was their honeymoon trip.

In *Singin' in the Rain*, Cyd got to dance a *pas de deux* with Gene Kelly. It was one of the most sensual, yet beautiful dances the censors would allow at that time. The dance number catapulted Cyd into stardom. Her next assignment was *Brigadoon*, in which she shared equal billing with Gene Kelly.

MGM's next big project was a musical, *The Band Wagon*, starring Fred Astaire. Fred thought Cyd Charisse would be an ideal partner for him, if she weren't so tall. Cyd heard about his concern and was devastated, since it had been her dream to dance with Fred Astaire.

One morning when Cyd was working out in the rehearsal hall, she could see Fred Astaire in the mirror coming toward her. She quickly dropped into a *demiplie,* French for a half-knee bend. Cyd remained in her bent knee position. Fred casually walked around, checking out her height from every angle, and then left. A short time later, the phone rang. It was Arthur Freed, the producer. He almost shouted, "Cyd, Fred thinks you're perfect for the part." Cyd was so relieved: she could finally stand up straight again. After the film was finished, Fred remarked that "dancing with Cyd is like floating on a cloud."

I first worked with Cyd on *Party Girl*, a gangster film that had several dance numbers in it. We had just begun rehearsals when the Musicians Guild went on strike. Since we had no music to rehearse with, we had to choreograph to spoken dancer's counts: "one and two and three and four", repeated *ad infinitum.* It was very difficult and taxing for Cyd and me, especially Cyd because she had to listen to my gravel voice counting. So I brought in four male dancers and gave them each a tom-tom drum. They supplied our music by beating the drums evenly to the count. That worked beautifully for us, until a delegate from the Musicians Guild came around and accused us of using musicians – namely drummers. Cyd suggested that when we showed him the number, I should tell the boys on the fourth count to roll their heads around as only dancers can do, as if their heads were detached from their bodies. We invited the delegate to the set, and Cyd very graciously performed the number with the four dancers. When the number was finished, I asked the delegate, "Now can any of your musicians do that with their heads?" He said, "Absolutely not. Those are dancers for sure." Cyd winked at me while thanking the delegate for visiting us. Working under those conditions cemented a strong friendship between Cyd and me, especially since the numbers turned out quite well. Eventually, Andre Previn composed music to the film. I worked with Cyd again on the film *The Silencer* starring Dean Martin.

One day, Tony Martin asked me if I would create a nightclub act for him and Cyd. I thought it was a great idea and I looked forward to working with the two of them at the same time. I had recently worked with Cyd and I had also done an Irving Berlin special, *A Salute to America*, starring Dinah Shore and Tony Martin, so I was sure I knew them well enough to be a referee, if necessary. I left the billing up to them; I didn't want to get in the way of anyone's ego. The act was constructed in two parts. Tony or Cyd each performed their own material and never shared the stage together until the end of the show, when they did a very funny "show biz" husband and wife bit we called *A Night at Home with the Martins*.

Both Cyd and I opted to try out the act before the opening in Las Vegas at the Riviera Hotel. Tony insisted we open without a tryout. I thought that was a risky business. After all, Cyd had never appeared on a stage other than when she danced with the Ballet Russe de Monte Carlo, which is quite different from appearing on a nightclub stage in front of a less cultured audience, more accustomed to belly laughs than to ballet turns. Cyd amazed me. She performed as though she had Tony's extensive experience in nightclubs.

The act encouraged Cyd to try the theatre. She played in the musicals *Charlie Boy* in London and *Grand Hotel* on Broadway. When she was asked to do a lecture tour, I convinced her to do it. I helped and coached her. Speaking in front of an audience is quite different from playing a part in a show or a club. As a lecturer, one doesn't have the luxury of the footlights to protect oneself. You're on your own. However, Cyd was very comfortable on her own. She's since performed in many television specials and talk shows. The shy little girl from Amarillo has certainly come a long way.

Unquestionably, Cyd Charisse is one of the most glamorous entertainers in the business. When she enters a room, both men and women stop to stare and ultimately approve. Her poise and elegance are seductive. Cyd can wrap a beach towel around her and look as though she's wearing the most expensive import from Paris. She is the one star for whom designers dream to create.

I often wish the Academy Awards production staff would invite Cyd to teach some of the female presenters how to walk across a stage and how to wear those expensive gowns. If nothing else, it would give the Academy Awards® Show some much needed "Charisse glamour".

Betty Hutton

Betty Hutton once said, "Applause was far more satisfying than sex." She said it and she believed it. She was totally consumed by show business. If you ever see the film *Annie Get Your Gun* and watch Betty while she's singing *There's No Business Like Show Business*, you'll suddenly sense that she's no longer on the screen. It's as if she's standing right in front of you. She sings it with such intensity and such fervor, you forget you're watching a movie.

Betty Hutton once created a great furor in New York City when she appeared in a musical called *Panama Hattie*. It starred the first lady of Broadway, Ethel Merman, who could do no wrong as far as the critics were concerned. Betty almost dethroned Ethel on opening night when she stopped the show so solidly that it had a problem continuing.

Betty's career took off after *Panama Hattie* and she ended up in Hollywood at Paramount Studios. In a very short time, she became one of their biggest stars and had the unusual ability to tackle any assignment with that fervor and enthusiasm that almost made you tired watching her. In *The Greatest Show On Earth*, Betty plays an aerialist and all the tricks you see performed are done by her and not a double. Cecil B. DeMille was very impressed with her talent and actually threw the picture her way. So she ended up with one of the best parts in the film and consequently got the best reviews.

I first met Betty Hutton when she interviewed me about directing and producing a nightclub act for her. She liked my ideas and we agreed that I would do it. I stipulated in my contract that the first three days of rehearsal were to be without her. I was to work with her singing/dancing group and then after the third day she would come in and see what we had done. We were in rehearsal on our second day and suddenly she popped up as if by magic and there she was by the stage. I never knew where she came from. As she explained later, she had watched the rehearsal from the floor and crawled to the stage when I saw her. She screamed, "It's wonderful! I want to start rehearsals right now, I'm ready!"

Betty was a very unpredictable person; you never knew what she was going to do next. We tried the act out in Scottsdale, Arizona. In the act, there was a sketch that she did with a boy. I didn't think the material was particularly funny, but it was an old burlesque bit that Betty was familiar with. Anyway, on opening night when Betty and the boy were doing the sketch, she stopped the entire performance and said, "No it's not getting the laughs it should get." She called me out and said, "Bob come on out and show him how to do it." There I was in the wings in my T-shirt. I was embarrassed, but had no choice other than to go on stage and do the sketch. When it was over the audience did laugh, not at my comedic efforts, they just laughed at the situation. However, you could never convince Betty that that was the case. The opening in Las Vegas of her nightclub act was a huge success and rightfully so, because Betty was really one of the very, very talented stars Hollywood ever produced. She played to packed houses and when she finished the engagement, that was it – she didn't want to go back again. She had proven that she was very good and that was all that she wanted to do.

I directed a TV pilot for Betty and NBC liked it. They were going to do a whole series for her. However, she insisted that the writer/producer be fired. Unfortunately, the writer/producer owned the show and so Betty said she wouldn't go on with him present and hence gave up a lot of money. But she couldn't care less; she had no conception of the value of money. If we were having a production meeting and one of her children, Candy or Lindsey, came in and just seemed to get in the way, she'd say, "Here" and give them a twenty dollar bill or whatever she had in her pocketbook and say, "Go buy yourself some chocolate." She was notorious for doing that. We were in a bar once and we each had a drink after rehearsal. I think in those days the bill came to like five dollars for the two of us. She handed me the money in her purse and said, "Give him twenty." "For what?" I said. "A tip." I said, "Betty you don't give a tip of twenty for a four dollar bill." She said, "Yes you do. He needs it more than I do."

Betty was extremely generous. She had a maid, Mary, a very nice, but very naive, woman. Mary always told Betty about these poor girls in her neighborhood who never had a place to sleep. So Betty gave her enough money to buy cots to put in her house for these poor gals. It turned out they were prostitutes and they just wanted a place to rest. But Betty didn't learn her lesson. Mary told Betty about a poor woman who had nothing, just a lot of children and Christmas was coming. So Betty had several of us go out and buy gifts. We arrived at the poor lady's house and there she was, surrounded by her five children. I'm sure that she didn't like any of the gifts we brought. They were useless for her - silk stockings, scarves, handkerchiefs. Betty even bought her a Vicuna bathrobe that probably cost enough to pay the woman's rent for a year. But there was nothing for the woman and children to eat. Betty looked at me and said, "You didn't bring any food," as though it were my fault. So as usual, someone else was responsible for Betty's indiscretions. The poor woman was so delighted when we did bring her some food. As we were leaving, I tried to tell the woman to see if she couldn't sell the Vicuna bathrobe and make some money on it, but Betty was standing too close to me.

Betty then did a TV series called *Goldie* that I directed. Over time, she got to the point where she had to do everything herself, even writing. Unfortunately, she couldn't sleep and depended on sleeping pills. It got so bad that she would take not one but three pills to fall asleep, and then she'd awake in the middle of the night and call me with all sorts of ideas for the next day's shoot. It became really exhausting, and I had had enough of it. However, that's show business and you put up with it. But Betty got to a stage of paranoia about the show and the end came when one day we were ready to shoot without her. She had called in saying she would be late and I was delighted because I could shoot around her and make some headway. Then she came in with a cast of actors that she had chosen and a script that she had worked on overnight. She said that that was what we were going to do. It was a total fiasco; it made absolutely no sense. And then Betty got a little discombobulated. She fired the camera director for laughing; she dismissed all the actors we had been working with. There were only two people left: the man who operated the camera and me. And finally she said to me, "I don't need you either" and she asked the man who ran the cameras, the operator, "What do you do?" and he tried to explain that he made the cameras work. She said, "We don't need you" and so he left too.

Unfortunately, after that, I think it was over for Betty in show business. Betty's paranoia had her always consumed with the thought that people didn't like her. For example, when she replaced Judy Garland in *Annie Get Your Gun*, she insisted that everybody at MGM

151

hated her because she had replaced Judy. But that was not the case. The people at MGM were delighted that she was there, if only because it meant they could work.

It was the same thing with her mother Mabel. Betty insisted that Mabel liked her sister Marion better than her. In fact Betty often said that her mother didn't like her at all. Well one night, poor Mabel, who smoked incessantly, fell asleep in her chair with a cigarette in her hand, which started a big fire. She did get out in time. But unfortunately she ran back into the apartment to retrieve something she had left there and the fumes and the flames got to her. When the firemen did find her she was on the floor and clutched to her heart was a framed photograph of Betty.

After Mabel's death, Betty turned to religion. Happily, she found a kindly wonderful priest called Father Tom who helped Betty understand that there was more to life than show business. Betty Hutton ended up working as a cleaning woman in a rectory. This would have made a wonderful film and Betty could have played the part beautifully, but she probably wouldn't have liked the script.

Pearl Bailey

It took three, six-foot stagehands to restrain Pearl Bailey from annihilating Ike Turner of the Ike and Tina Turner nightclub act. This melee occurred at an orchestra rehearsal of the *Pearl Bailey Show*, which I was staging. Ike and Tina were scheduled to go over their music at 11:00 a.m., a time he insisted upon. But 11:00 a.m. arrived and there was no Ike and Tina Turner. So I asked our conductor Louie Belson, who was Pearl's husband, to take some of the other acts and go over their music. He did, and then at 11:30 there was still no Ike and Tina Turner. So we rehearsed other parts of the show. Finally, after 12:00, when there was nothing else for the band to do, Pearl said, "Why don't you dismiss the band and give them a half-hour break, and we'll just stay and wait for those two to get here." She picked up her needles and wool and started to knit furiously. She stabbed at each stitch. All I could think of was Madame DeFarge in *A Tale of Two Cities*. I was certain that someone was going to catch hell.

A little after 1:00, Ike sauntered on stage, followed by a shy and embarrassed Tina Turner. On seeing them, Pearl announced loudly and deliberately, "You'd think some people would have better manners and would apologize when they're late." Ike interrupted her, and tauntingly said, "OK, we're late. Now what are you going to do about it?" Pearl darted out of her seat and she was on that stage in two seconds flat, and it was then that the crewmembers had to hold her back. What Ike Turner didn't know was that The Pearl Bailey Show represented the culmination of years of struggle, denial, frustration, prejudice, honky-tonk nightclubs, flea-ridden hotel rooms, and all the other vagaries of show business she had endured. That didn't keep Pearl from reaching the top. She was the first black female performer to have a television series of her own. It was her badge of honor. Her own little world populated by her dancers, her musicians, her technicians, her stage hands and her production staff, and no one was going to upset that apple cart. Certainly not Ike Turner.

After the Saturday night taping of the show, we had a feast of roast chickens, hams, salads – all prepared by Pearl herself, with the assistance of her maid. There was nothing that Pearl wouldn't do for her little family. However, she wasn't easy to work for. She expected 100% of your effort. And if you didn't give her 100%, that was it. You were finished.

There was one part of the show Pearl liked especially. It wasn't scripted – it was ad-libbed. She would interview one of her guests, and surprise them with questions they weren't ready for. This happened to Ethel Waters, the black diva of the American theater, whose image was unblemished. Apparently in the past, Ethel Waters must have offended Pearl or snubbed her, and Pearl was going to settle that old account with her on this show. She asked Ethel questions that would have annoyed another person. For example, she asked her, "you don't like children, do you?" But Ms. Waters was too clever for Pearl. However, Pearl's insistence and her sly innuendos finally got to Ms. Waters. When Pearl asked Ms. Waters, "have you ever stood in the way of the success of new talent that you were threatened by?" she exploded, betraying her staid image and showing her true self. She was just as much hellion as Pearl. The two of them went at each other and it was almost hysterically funny, because you thought they were going to tear each other's hair out at any moment. But that didn't happen. It turned out to be a delightful part of the program. However, when Ethel Waters left the theater, she never bothered to say goodbye to Pearl.

Pearl had an uncanny perception about other performers. She was never jealous of them. When they were good, she was the first to admit it. We once had Joan Rivers on our show, before she became a television star. At that time, she had made quite a name for herself back East in nightclubs. When she was on the show, Pearl had a comment after she saw her act. She said, "You know, this girl is going to go very far. Only because her material is based on smut and that's the sort of thing people like today," and dismissed Joan very curtly.

The one guest everyone was really looking forward to was Lucille Ball, because we all thought she and Pearl would make magic together. Lucy was brought on stage on a palanquin carried by four of the dancing boys, and they deposited her right next to Pearl. There was a script for the two of them to read, but apparently they decided to chuck the script and just ad lib and match wits. It would have worked, had one of the ladies backed down and been willing to be stooge to the other. But that didn't happen. Especially when Lucy said to Pearl, "Congratulations on

154

your new television series. Do you think it will last another season?" Neither one would give up her supreme position. And so the meeting was not very successful. In fact, as they knew they weren't getting laughs they kept parting from each other and stepping back, stepping back, until they were reading lines from either side of the stage. It was a sad disappointment to all of us, because we really thought that it could be fun. But it wasn't.

Pearl's big moment came when she was one of the performers in the grand benefit for the Motion Picture Home and the farewell to Frank Sinatra. Pearl was apparently on tour with *Hello, Dolly*. In her absence, I staged a number for her with six very promising chorus boys, namely: Jack Lemmon, Don Rickles, David Niven, Joe Namath, Sammy Davis, Jr. and Rock Hudson. Rehearsal with each one of them had to be separate, because they were all working people. Consequently, I never got to work with them as a group until this final rehearsal. When Pearl arrived the night of the show, this number, which will be remembered by anyone who was there, couldn't be followed. In fact, Frank Sinatra said to me, "If you put me on after that number, I'll kill you." And I realized that's what he meant. The number was hysterically funny. It was incredible, all these six hams on stage supposedly supporting Pearl, who in turn improvised bits with each one. It was really a brilliant performance. The great misfortune is that the benefit was never taped. Pearl was at her best. The only thing that could follow that number was intermission, and that's exactly what we had. Intermission.

Pearl never let on she had a bad heart, and that was one reason why she wouldn't renew her contract to do another season of television. All her life she was embarrassed that she had never had a proper education. So she moved to Washington, D.C., where she attended George Washington University. While there, she hobnobbed with some of her political friends – Richard and Pat Nixon, Gerald and Betty Ford, the Eisenhowers. She finally did get her degree and left us with a smile, because Pearl Bailey was a college graduate who happened to be a performer.

Mitzi Gaynor

Mitzi Gaynor has the distinction of being one Hollywood lady who turned down President John F. Kennedy. She said, "No, no, most definitely no." I know. I was there at The Latin Casino in Cherry Hill, New Jersey, where Mitzi's much acclaimed nightclub act was to play. She and her troupe arrived two days before opening because Mitzi is a perfectionist and she must try out the stage, her quick costume changes and even go over the act several times, an act she had been performing nightly for the past three months. She insisted I fly in from the Coast to supervise rehearsals since I had directed and choreographed the show and might want to make some changes.

Mitzi's act was to follow delightful Jimmy Durante and Peter Lawford, who were appearing at the Casino. Peter invited himself to our rehearsals, explaining that he was a big fan of Mitzi. He very casually asked me if I thought Mitzi would appear at a gala in Washington for the President. I told him I would discuss it with her and when I did, she said it was impossible. The gala would coincide with our opening in Detroit, her hometown, and she told me to explain to Peter that Detroit came first. He was astonished. He couldn't believe anyone would dare turn down the President. Later that afternoon, Peter came back with another offer, namely, "What if she were the only female performer at the gala?" I tried that offer on Mitzi and her answer was "No, no, definitely no." I told Peter to forget the gala. There was no way she would do it; but he insisted, "What if she were the *only* performer there?" Without losing a beat, I said, "Peter, stop pimping for the President."

We did keep our date in Detroit and she played to sell-out houses even though there wasn't one person Mitzi knew there. That didn't matter: Mitzi was home and that did matter.

At the time of the President Kennedy incident, Mitzi had already been exposed to the machinations of high-positioned predators of lovely young women. She had met and been seduced by the master of them all, Howard Hughes. Hughes's fetish was women's breasts. Mitzi, handily, met that qualification and had much more than that going for her. She had been on her way to stardom before she met Howard Hughes;

therefore, the scripted dialogue "I can make you a star" wouldn't work. So the master of them all had to assume the role of the love-smitten male. His campaign, however, had the advantage of unlimited funds, airplanes, limousines, flowers, jewels and all the amenities that would impress any woman, let alone Mitzi who wasn't quite out of her teens. Mitzi was in love. True, she had heard rumors about his many affairs, but that didn't trouble her. Hughes had told her he wanted to marry her, which was as likely as Hitler marrying Fanny Brice. When Mitzi discovered there were many girls around town he had promised to marry too, she made her exit and left the enigmatic Howard Hughes for good. She chose a more reliable partner, Jack Bean, who became her agent, her manager, her producer, her lover and her husband.

Mitzi was born in Chicago. When she was three, her family moved to Detroit. As a child Mitzi was very shy, withdrawn, and always lost in reverie. Her distraught mother decided Mitzi should take dancing lessons, because, as every wise mother knows, dancing class could do more for a troubled child than chicken soup could do for the common cold.

Mitzi was enrolled in Madame Etienne's School of Ballet. Madame Etienne, one of the renowned Charisse dancing family, took to her new pupil instantly and became Mitzi's second mother, theatrically that is. Mitzi blossomed in class. The dance studio became her playground, her happy world.

On one momentous day, Madame Etienne announced, prophetically and without the aid of a crystal ball, that Mitzi would become a great movie star. Mitzi's mother went right out and bought two tickets for Hollywood. It wasn't long before Madame and the Etienne School of Ballet took off for "tinsel town" too, with the assurance that her new school would have at least one pupil, her darling Mitzi.

Mitzi had a fragmentary education, always being one step ahead of the truant officer. While most kids were in school struggling with algebra, Mitzi was appearing nightly on stage in one of the legendary Los Angeles City Light Opera productions, at the age of 14. Her education, while not traditional, was invaluable. Her teachers were some of the greats in musical theatre. Her awesome flair for comedy must have been inspired by several of the incomparable comedians she watched so intensely from the wings. Mitzi is familiar with the "shticks" and tricks comedians use while "selling" their art. She has an incredible memory and she is a walking lexicon of theatre history.

It was inevitable that a talent scout would discover and bring this bubbling bundle of talent to the attention of the casting director at Twentieth Century Fox. In her first film, she was given the second female lead in *My Blue Heaven*, starring her idol, Betty Grable. I first met Mitzi when I was signed to choreograph and stage the musical numbers in a low-budget film called *Bloodhounds on Broadway*, based on a Damon Runyon story. The film was a "sleeper", a box office success and it deservedly made Mitzi a star. It was then when Howard Hughes heard about this newcomer, ran film on her, saw what he liked, and almost immediately went on the prowl.

After the Hughes affair, Mitzi worked tirelessly from one film to another. She partnered with such giants as Gene Kelly, Donald O'Connor and Dan Dailey. In non-musical films, she played opposite Frank Sinatra, Kirk Douglas, David Niven and Yul Brynner. Mitzi reached the heights as an actress in *South Pacific*. Her portrayal of nurse Nellie Forbish is a most sensitive and tender performance, Oscar quality.

Mitzi's first nightclub act at the Flamingo Hotel in Las Vegas was a monumental success, the best ticket in town, and it played to packed houses nightly. Even after Christmas and New Year's, when usually there's very little business in that city, she was a sell-out. The Sands Hotel, at three-night intervals, played some of their biggest stars against her – Frank Sinatra, Dean Martin and Jerry Lewis, Red Skelton, Joey Bishop – yet she drew the crowds. After Las Vegas, Mitzi was booked to play the Deauville in Miami, the sister hotel to the Las Vegas Flamingo. Again, Mitzi was the talk of the city.

We were there only a few nights when the Ed Sullivan Show arranged to tape and use our opening number as part of their show. The rest of the Sullivan Show was to perform on a platform in the hotel's ballroom. Panic set in when the CBS technicians couldn't pipe the electrical cables into our stage. As a concession to Ed Sullivan, it was agreed Mitzi would do our opening number on the improvised platform and then return to the theatre and start our regular show. However, I insisted we needed fifteen minutes to make the necessary adjustments and changes in our routine because the platform was half the size of the space we were accustomed to. When I got to the room with the platform, there was a girl on it with her back to me. She was wearing Bermuda shorts and wore her hair in a stylish bob. She was strumming a ukulele. I shouted to the stage manager "Get that girl off the platform" and he shouted back at me, "That's one of the Beatles." I screamed, "I don't care who she is, get her off." Paul McCartney in his Bermuda shorts and his well-shaped legs with his back to me looked like a girl. Incidentally, the Beatles made their American debut on that Sullivan show.

Mitzi and her troupe managed the damned platform brilliantly. After the number was over, I was convinced Mitzi could perform on a postage stamp if she had to.

Joseph Pasternak

If you saw him puttering about in the kitchen, hopping about from one pot to another while announcing, "You must stir it occasionally and be sure to add paprika, lots of paprika, because Hungarian cooking without paprika does not make it," you'd think you were watching a new cooking show on television. Not so! You were watching one of MGM foremost producers, Joe Pasternak, at home in his kitchen. He loved the kitchen because it was a refuge for him where he could unwind after a rough day at the studio. It also had a lot to do with his early beginnings.

When Joe Pasternak arrived in this country from Hungary, he was a very young man. He was interested in filmmaking, so he ended up in Hollywood where he got a job at Universal Studios working as a waiter in the commissary. Joe must have waited on the right people, because it wasn't long before he was given a job working in the production department. On his own, without too much help from anyone, he quickly ended up as a producer. His great contribution to Universal was his wonderful discovery of Deanna Durbin, a young teenager with a magnificent voice. She became number one at the box office, which helped Universal financially.

Unfortunately, Universal didn't have many musical performers under contract. So when MGM offered Joe a job, he took it quickly because he knew there was a lot of musical talent at that studio. And since his interest in the film industry was musicals, that was the place to be. At MGM, he proved to be an innovator when he brought in his pictures on very low budgets, but of good quality. That pleased the production department immensely and Joe became one of the reigning heads in MGM's hierarchy.

I worked on several films for Joe –*Where the Boys Are, Please Don't Eat the Daisies, Looking for Love, Party Girl* and *The Opposite Sex*. I found him to be a most agreeable person to work for. He did not push his weight around. He was very understanding. If you did anything that he liked, he'd tell you that immediately. If you didn't, he'd also gently explain why he didn't. He was a joy to be with.

There was a big production number in *The Opposite Sex* and it was not to be performed by one of the characters in the film but by an outside performer. Joe asked me to look at some film that someone had sent him. It was film of a young man who had become a sensation back East and this was an appearance he made on *The Ed Sullivan Show*. We watched the film but unfortunately all we could see was his upper body. Everything below was censored and it was obvious that there must have been a lot of gyrations and bumps going on somewhere below his tonsils. But I explained to Joe, "If television censored his performance, the film censors would just kill us if we used it. We would never get the number to make any sense if we did the whole thing in close-up on this man's face." So I recommended a young, talented, song and dance man called Jerry Antes. The young man we didn't use was Elvis Presley. Joe was offered ten percent of Elvis' career if he used him in the film, which would represent a considerable fortune. However, Joe never once reproached me for my recommendation. I must admit, to this day I have not lived that down. But Joe said, "You win some, you lose some."

When he was asked to produce the Academy Awards® show, Joe called me and said, "I want you to be my co-producer because I know you've worked on some of the shows and you have good taste and good judgment." The phrase "good judgment" made me shudder, thinking back to Elvis Presley. But Joe didn't mean that at all. The Academy Awards show was fun. We enjoyed doing it and as is usual, everyone said it was the best show ever!

Joe, his lovely wife, Dorothy, and I were good friends and often we'd be in Vegas. Joe's pretext was, as he said, that he'd like to see the act I had just done for someone up there. Actually, the reason he wanted to be in Vegas was because he loved the roulette table where he always won. Even if he lost he'd say he won. Just as when back at their house we would play Scrabble, he had to win, even if it meant inventing words that never existed in Webster's Dictionary. It was typical of his Napoleonic complex. Joe was a short man, but he had a big heart and big talent.

The Pasternaks' home in Bel Air was a lovely mansion where every evening at cocktail time people would drop in and have a drink and just stay for a while. It was a wonderful meeting place. Joe and Dorothy did give big parties, but the best one they ever gave happened on New

161

Year's Eve. Dorothy decided on this particular New Year's Eve that they would just have a few friends over and a very casual evening spent with drinks and food – a sane evening, welcoming the New Year as intelligent people should. And we were all there, her special guests, sitting there, enjoying the party, drinks and small talk, when we heard fire engines going back and forth. Someone turned on the radio and it was announced that there was a tremendous fire in the Bel Air hills. Just then, the doorbell rang. Dorothy went to the door thinking it was the fire department telling us to evacuate. But it was David Niven and Laurence Olivier. They explained, after apologizing, that the fire kept them from going to the party they were expected at and had come to join us. Dorothy said, "Well come in, welcome, be our guests, join the group." No sooner had they settled with a drink when the doorbell rang again and this time it was Rita Hayworth and Freddie Karger. They too had a similar problem; the roads were barricaded to where they wanted to go. This kept going on all evening until at one point this party that was supposed to be very quiet, turned into a rather loud, well-dressed group of people that you'd expect to see at the Beverly Hills Hotel celebrating the New Year.

Guests arrived constantly. The champagne flowed easily, so there was no problem. Everyone was feeling quite good. There were many celebrities in the crowd. You could see Elizabeth Taylor and her latest swain; Judy Garland and Chuck Walters; Cyd Charisse and Tony Martin; Jack Benny and Mary Livingston; Jean Simmons and Richard Brooks; Angie Dickinson and Burt Bacharach. It seemed more like the Governor's Ball reception after an Academy Awards® evening. The problem I worried about was food. How on earth could they possibly feed this huge a crowd? But Joe and his household staff rose to the occasion admirably. Under Joe's supervision, they whipped up one dish after another, remembering to add paprika. The buffet table never looked empty because as one platter was finished, another replaced it. Poor Joe, he had to supervise the kitchen and also act as host. But he handled both assignments brilliantly. The evening never seemed to end, people stayed on forever. Finally, in the wee hours, the last guest left.

I phoned Dorothy and Joe the next day to thank them for a very interesting, improvised party and I asked them how they held up. Joe said, "We're fine. We enjoyed it immensely. Even if we had planned a party like that, we couldn't have done it so well." He said, "But you know the party was very valuable for me because it's given me a wonderful idea for a new cookbook and I have the right title for it. I'm going to call the book, *Recipes for Uninvited Guests.*"

Susan Hayward

Both Michael Woulfe, who was the head costume designer at RKO, and I arrived at the home of Susan Hayward. We were to meet with her concerning the film *The Conqueror*. As Michael reached for the doorbell, the door opened and there she was, the lady herself, Miss Hayward. She had been apprised of Michael Woulfe's visit and she was ready for him. However, she was a little annoyed to find someone else present. She immediately demanded, "Who is that?" Michael Woulfe explained, "That's Bob Sidney, he's the choreographer on the picture." She shot back, "Oh, so they expect me to dance, do they?" And I said, meekly, "Can you?" She glowered at me, as if to say, "You're in for real trouble."

She ushered us into the living room, turned again toward me, and said, "Now what about this dance in the script?" And I said, "Miss Hayward, you really don't have to worry about the dance in the script. We have arranged for a very talented dancer who will do the number for you. All we need from you are two close-ups. One where you see the dagger and the other where you throw it at John Wayne." Then, she attacked Michael and said, "Where are your sketches?" She then discarded one after another, saying: "This won't do", "It's all wrong", "It could be better", and "I don't like this". I deliberately picked up one from the floor and said, "Michael, this one is just fabulous for the dance number. Please remember it." She then ushered us to the door after glowering at me once again.

On the way home, I felt sorry for Michael and told him that he needn't be too upset, because the sketches really were excellent, and it was widely known that Susan Hayward wanted no part of the picture *The Conqueror*. In fact, she turned it down at her studio, Twentieth Century Fox. Howard Hughes at RKO insisted that she play the part. And so Twentieth Century Fox threatened to put her on suspension if she didn't take the assignment. Susan Hayward had a fairly pragmatic attitude about money and said she would do the film. *The Conqueror*, at the outset, was very ridiculous. You couldn't blame Susan Hayward. It was the story of Ghengis Khan, the marauding Mongol warrior, who conquered most of Asia Minor. To give it authenticity, the author wrote it in biblical style. In typical Hollywood fashion, they cast John Wayne, with his Midwestern monotone as Ghengis Khan. They had Pedro Armandades, a very talented Mexican actor, with his Mexican accent, playing John Wayne's brother; and for John Wayne's mother they used Agnes Moorehead, who sounded like she was the President of the Ladies Luncheon Club. In any event, the film was done seriously, although I think it could have made a great comedy.

Susan Hayward was very difficult from the moment she started the picture. She was uncooperative with all of the department heads, because she didn't want to do the picture. One day, she arrived on the dance stage. She came in and very abruptly said, "I've come to see the dance number." I said, "Oh, Miss Hayward, you needn't worry about it. As I told you earlier, we have a very talented dancer and she'll do the number for you. All we need is a close-up of you looking at the dagger and then a second close-up of you throwing the dagger." She said, "I said I want to see the number," with great finality. So we showed it to her. When it was over, she kicked off the slippers she was wearing and said, "Let's rehearse." Both my dancer and I couldn't believe what we had heard.

Susan worked hard. She put all of her energy into learning the number. I must say that when you see it on the screen, most people think she was a trained dancer. She really wasn't. It was a delight to work with her because I admired her courage and her tenacity. She would never stop for a break. She kept going tirelessly. We all loved her at the end.

Susan and I became immediate friends. We'd laugh about things the picture was doing and what was happening with it. Actually, one day I came on the set to see how they were doing. John Wayne had a scene with her where he grabs her and shakes her. They yelled, "Cut!" and she came over to me because the hairpiece she was wearing had flown off, he was shaking her so strongly. She said, "He's hurting me. Look at me, I'm black and blue. What do I do?" I said, "Susan, I'll go to him. In the next take, if he doesn't behave, just raise your knee." Well, I went to John and said, "You know she's rather delicate and we need her for the dance number. She can't be bruised." He said, "Well, she's fighting me and no woman can do that," in his John Wayne monotone. I went right back to Susan and said, "The minute the shot begins and he grabs you, raise your knee right in the proper place." She did and they actually yelled, "Cut!" because John Wayne was hopping about trying desperately to breathe. For about five minutes he sounded like a soprano.

The Conqueror was filmed in St. George, Utah, near where the U.S. Army was conducting secret nuclear tests. It is believed that the cast was exposed to the fallout of radioactive material from the tests, because Susan, John Wayne, Pedro Armandades, Agnes Moorehead, Dick Powell, the film's director, Susan's wardrobe woman, and several other cast and crewmembers all died of cancer. Somehow I escaped their fate, even though I was up there for a four-day visit to go over something with Dick Powell and, gratefully, I came back and am still here.

Susan developed her friendship with me based on work. It was not a social one entirely, but she would often ask my advice on certain things. In fact, she sent for me on a picture she was doing. There was a scene they had asked her to perform and she didn't like the way the director had done it. She had her own idea of how it should play and wanted it her way. So she asked me to come on the set. I thought, at first, that she wanted me to come on as a visitor. In front of the director, she did both his version and her version and asked me what I thought. Quite truthfully, had I been the director, I would have thrown the intruder out immediately. But the director was absolutely right, and I told that to Susan. She asked if I was telling her the truth. I said, "Susan, would I lie?" I sheepishly left the set, embarrassed to be put in that position.

When we were doing *Valley of the Dolls*, poor Judy Garland was replaced and they used Susan Hayward instead. It was a good part for Susan. There was a song that she was to perform. Margaret Whiting sang the song and Susan had to lip sync to it, as we do in films. She did it so well and with such energy that people thought she was singing the song herself. It was very convincing. I worked with her throughout the picture as usual. We got along beautifully and she was a joy to work with. However, she did have a little problem with Patty Duke, who behaved like the wild little teenager she was. That didn't faze Susan. Nothing got in her way.

One day at Twentieth Century Fox, I had a call from Jerry Wald. He was the most important producer on the lot at that time. He was going to do a television series and he wanted Susan to play the lead, because it would be prestigious for Fox to have a star of her magnitude on television. She said she would only play it if I were the director. He said to me, "I really don't want you. You're a very respected choreographer. But you don't have experience as a director, and I can have my pick of the best directors in town. But unless you're the director, Susan won't take the job. So the job is yours." We never got to work on the series, because sadly, Susan died two days later of brain cancer.

I shall always remember her kindness and her faith in me. Susan was one of those people to whom it didn't matter whether you were important or unimportant. She would risk working with anyone in whom she believed and who could get the job done. She was an unusual lady. I'm very fortunate to have worked with some special people in this business, and Susan Hayward was one of the most special.

Dean Martin

When Dean Martin and Jerry Lewis first invaded Hollywood after their incredibly successful nightclub appearances, Paramount Studios signed them to make a film called *Jumping Jacks*, and also gave them the run of the place. Jerry and Dean did just that: they ran away with the place. The shenanigans the two perpetrated on set were unbelievable. It was nothing for Jerry to throw a forward pass to Dean right through the lights, with some football he found on the lot, thus endangering the lives of everyone present. Or Jerry might stop a take right in the middle of a good scene because he wanted to tell a joke to everyone on the sidelines. Jerry didn't know that when you are making a movie in Hollywood, comedy is best played to the aperture of the camera, not to the onlookers.

Jerry totally dominated Dean, just as he did in their nightclub act. In fact, Dean was really a stooge for Jerry's comedy. Dean never got to finish a song during the act, because if he started to sing, Jerry would come and interrupt him with all sorts of antics. Most audiences didn't know of Dean's wonderful singing voice until later on in his career. But during the film, Jerry did worry about Dean's welfare. Before a take, he would go over Dean's make-up; he would fix his tie and straighten his hair. He would behave like a mother hen clucking over her chicks. I was signed to choreograph and stage the musical numbers for *Jumping Jacks*. I suspect that Paramount chose me because they knew that I had staged and choreographed Irving Berlin's *This Is The Army*, and they thought we could make this into another military epic, which was so far from reality.

In any case, when I worked with Dean away from Jerry, I realized that, in addition to having a charming voice, he was a very gifted comedian. His brand of comedy was not the overt kind that Jerry's was. Jerry's idea of comedy would be to imitate a paraplegic by walking on his ankles. That sort of humor never amused me.

Shortly after the picture was finished, Martin and Lewis split up. Jerry's prediction that Dean would never be able to survive without him couldn't have been further from the truth. Later, Dean played the lead in a picture called *The Silencers*, which was Columbia Pictures' version of the

James Bond movies. *The Silencers* was not a great hit; however, it was a wonderful vehicle for Dean because he came through with a strong persona. He didn't play the part the way Sean Connery or Roger Moore did – very casual and off-hand, where they would snap their fingers and a beautiful girl would appear. No, Dean played it more like a mischievous brat. He had a wonderful boyish quality that shone from the screen. Both women and men responded well to him.

My work on the picture was to stage a number for Cyd Charisse, who, according to the plot, gets killed in the beginning. I got to see Dean again and would hang around his dressing room when I had nothing to do. One day, they were doing a scene where they wanted Dean to bare his chest. He was hesitant to do it. I went to his dressing room and gave him a real back-stage pep talk. I told him, "Get out there. You've got a great body, why not show it? Everybody else would if they were in your place." He finally did, although he was embarrassed. But it worked for him. Dean did it his way. He performed it like a strip tease – undoing his shirt one seductive button at a time, bearing one shoulder, then the other, and finally turning his back to the audience when the shirt was off. Everyone on the sidelines was hysterical, until the director yelled, "Cut! Ok, Dean, you can play the scene with or without your shirt on. Do whatever you want."

After *The Silencers*, he played one of the leads in *Murderer's Row* and *The Ambushers*. They weren't box office smashes either, but they were important for Dean, because he had established himself as a leading man and a star. In fact, when Dean, Bing Crosby and Mitzi Gaynor were guests on the Frank Sinatra Timex Special, Mitzi said that Dean was "delightful, delicious and delovely (borrowing from Cole Porter), the perfect gent and heaven to work with." Even performing with such stiff competition as Crosby and Sinatra, Dean held his own and established himself as a very strong television personality. So much so that, along with his other credits, NBC signed Dean to a two-year contract to do a musical hour on television.

I joined *The Dean Martin Show* in its second year. I staged musical numbers, sketches and anything else that was needed. When I joined the show, the ratings were about 17. After my third week, they were 7, and then 3 and 2. For the remainder of my run there, we were always number 1 or 2. Lee Hale, who took care of the vocals, worked with me and we would pretty much put together the whole show. Dean only showed up on the day of the performance; he never came to rehearsals. On the day of the performance, he would watch a run-through with myself or Lee doing his part. He would then go out and do it live in front of the audience with whomever the star was that week. Like Dean, our director/producer Greg Garrison only showed up two days before the performance. He would have a run-through so he could familiarize himself with the show, and that was the extent of his creative contribution. Dean never knew that. No more than he knew about his finances, where all he cared about was that if he wanted new golf clubs or a new car, he could have it. Just as with the show, he only needed to know that everything was in order. He knew that the show had good ratings and that his henchmen were around him, and that was good enough.

Television was the ideal medium for Dean's personality. He was free of Jerry Lewis. He had come out of his social cocoon. He was on his own. He handled his visiting artists brilliantly. He never once tried to upstage his performers on the show. In fact, he helped launch some stars. Dom DeLuise appeared as a guest early in his career as a promising young comedian. He brought with him a sketch called Dominic the Great, in which he plays a knife thrower. His assistant, Giuseppi, would stand in front of a board and have Dom throw knives at several points around his body. He used one of the singers to play Giuseppi during the run-through. The night of the show, when Dom said, "Ladies and Gentlemen, my assistant – Giuseppi," instead of the singer, Dean walked out. Dom almost fell over laughing, as did the audience who were in on it.

The second time Dom appeared on the show, he had more stature and wasn't so apologetic. He brought a sketch in which he plays a waiter in a nightclub, serving two guests. It was a scene in which everything went wrong – he drops things, puts napkins around Dean's neck, the typical mishaps that happen in a restaurant. He said, "I need Dean to play the part of one of the guests." By the third time he was on the show, he said with newfound assurance, "Dean, this is your part." Dom had now arrived and become a star. However, he was always so grateful to Dean because he knew that Dean had made his career happen.

Dean also helped Florence Henderson reach stardom. The first time she was on the show, she had something of a reputation for playing the ingenue. She had performed several roles on Broadway and had a beautiful singing voice. But Dean sensed that she could be funny and he played up to it. They got a lot of laughs together and Florence was invited back to the show about four times after that. By the time of her last appearance, she was established enough to get the lead part in *The Brady Bunch*.

Dean did much for Joey Heatherton, too. He appreciated, along with many others in the business, that this bombshell would be the logical successor to Marilyn Monroe. Dean played opposite her beautifully, especially when they did a duet. He made it hysterically funny. In Joey Heatherton's case she too gained strong recognition, so much so that she got the lead in the Dean Martin Summer Show *The Golddiggers* with Frank Sinatra, Jr. in 1968. Dean really catapulted her career into motion. But, unfortunately, some artists get lost on the way and get on the wrong bus. That may have been the case with Joey, whom I still think could have been one of our most important young performers. There's a glimmer of hope for Joey, because her monumental talents cannot be denied. Some of the powers that be have begun to realize that there was more to Ms. Heatherton than her beauty. Her extraordinary voice is finally being recognized and acknowledged. If she can wade through the machinations of the recording industry, Joey's career as a vocal artist should be reborn.

When Don Rickles was on the show, even though he had never appeared on television before, Dean knew just what to do with him. He played up to Don's strengths, so that he was as comfortable and brilliant on television as he was in a nightclub. Dean did that for many performers. He handled a sketch brilliantly. He was a great leveler. When Orson Welles, who was very pompous and grand, was on the show, Dean after about two or three ad-lib lines got Orson to laugh and almost become quite human. Dean and Jimmy Stewart together were hysterically funny, because Jimmy couldn't keep a straight face when he was working with Dean, and Dean loved it when his guests would break up. And Jimmy did just that; they were both like mischievous boys.

Dean had many beautiful ladies and talented artists on the show. He treated them with great respect. In the case of Petula Clark, when she went through her music during orchestra rehearsal on the day of the show, Dean came out of his dressing room and stood on stage to listen to her, something he had never done before. After the run-through, I went to Petula Clark's dressing room to give her a few notes. There was a polite rap on the door and Dean walked in. He was very embarrassed when he saw me there. His weak excuse was, "I, I, I was wondering if you need anything, Petula. I'd be very happy to make sure you get it." And he was awkward; he just disappeared. That was very unlike Dean. I don't think he ever went to anyone's dressing room. It was obvious that Petula Clark got to him. But that's as far as it went. During the show, Petula and Dean did their duet on a divan with a lot of pillows. It was like a bed. Dean looked at her like a lovesick puppy. Petula then took the pillows and started hitting him, and the two of them ended up in a pillow fight. That was the end of the romance.

One of Dean's favorite performers was Caterina Valenti, the international singing star. She sang in twelve languages and spoke seven – French, Italian, Spanish, German, Portuguese, Russian and English. Dean was in awe of her musical talent. Not only could Caterina sing beautifully, she also played several musical instruments. Caterina found Dean to be one of the most humorous people she worked with. She couldn't go through one of their duets they sang together without laughing, desperately trying to maintain her composure. The two of them made magic on the screen. She definitely was one of the best guests we ever had on the show.

When Frank Sinatra was on the show, he and Dean together made history, because the two of them were so outrageous. They never stuck to the script. Dean's one ad-lib broke up Frank when he said, "It's allright, I'll be your stooge. I used to do that once in a nightclub act with a certain partner I had." Poor Frank couldn't go on. He couldn't continue singing.

I have another fond memory of Dean that happened when I was visiting a friend in Texas who was a big Dean Martin fan. No sooner had I arrived when he bundled me off and told me that we were going on a surprise trip. We drove for hours and hours, until finally we arrived in Breckenridge, Texas, a ghost-town in no-man's land. On the outskirts of town, I could see a movie set. They were shooting a western starring Dean. That was the surprise. There was Dean, bored out of his skull with nothing to do. I got out of the car, and Dean did a double-take. "Bob, is that you? What the hell are you doing out here in the middle of nowhere?" I told him, "Oh, I was just passing by." He laughed. He was so happy to see an old friend, that we stayed a couple of days and had a lot of fun relieving his boredom. He even pleased my friend by posing for photos with him. He showed us some rope tricks he had learned. Dean loved the riding sequences and learned to ride very well. He seemed to enjoy being away from the craziness of the studios and his Beverly Hills haunts. He was happier and more relaxed wearing his western gear and riding horses than he was doing his television show in black tie. At one point, I asked if he wanted me to study his lines with him. But he refused, laughing, "I have enough problems without your help, thank you." Actually, he didn't need my help. He knew his lines perfectly when he arrived on the set. Dean was a real professional and knew that unlike television, where he could improvise, with film he had to stick to the script. He was a director's delight.

The Dean Martin we all knew seemed to be so open, yet I doubt that anyone really knew him. As Dean Martin's daughter Gail once said to me, "I doubt that my Dad really knew who he was himself." Although he always had a drink in one hand and a lit cigarette in the other on the show, Dean didn't drink or smoke as much as people thought. Most of that was for effect. We did know this about Dean. When his son Dino, who was a flight officer, was in a plane crash that ended his life, nothing mattered to Dean any more, neither show business nor his social life. He just sank lower and lower, until finally he, too, left us. But, fortunately, he also left us with a wealth of tapes of his performances and his records, so that Dean's warmth, talent and charm will always be with us.

Irving Berlin

It happened after a performance of Irving Berlin's *This Is The Army* at the London Palladium during the Second World War. Irving Berlin – we soldiers called him "Mr. B" – burst into my dressing room in a panic, out of breath, hoarsely shouting … "it happened … I can't believe it … but it happened … the King and Queen asked to meet me! … me Izzy Baline … the little Jewish songwriter from the Lower East Side … they asked to meet me!" It was true, King George VI and his Queen Elizabeth saw *This Is The Army* that night and they graciously invited Mr. B to their box to tell him how much they enjoyed the show and how pleased they were to learn that all the monies earned in England would go to the British War Charities. I was very uncomfortable to see him toadying to anyone, even "The Royals." After all, Irving Berlin was the musical giant of Tin Pan Alley. We slavishly revered him, his genius and, most importantly, his creation of *This Is The Army*, which made it possible for actors, singers and dancers to be part of the war effort and to do what they did best - perform. That night back at our improvised barracks, I couldn't sleep. It wasn't the air raid going on. Air raids were almost a nightly occurrence those days in London, and it was wise to ignore them and go about one's business. I suddenly realized what kept me awake. It was a story Hassard Short, the formidable producer of all the Berlin shows at the Music Box Theatre, told me.

It was a simple love story. Irving Berlin courted and married Ellin Mackay, daughter of the communications czar John Mackay, the C.E.O. of Western Union, who was as prejudiced as he was gauche. He couldn't and wouldn't accept that his daughter would marry the immigrant Jewish songwriter Irving Berlin (the name was now Berlin, no longer Baline). Mackay conveniently forgot that he himself was descended from a long line of bricklayers who did well if they could spell their name. He was vindictive. He hired spies to spread vicious lies about Berlin. The young couple couldn't go anywhere without cameras glaring at them. Hassard Short suggested the two leave the country if only to retain their sanity and he volunteered to accompany them to Bermuda. The calm and serenity of the island would be the respite they needed from the unrelenting invasion of their privacy and what better background for the honeymoon they never had than Bermuda. The ship had no sooner entered the harbor when they were informed that reporters, photographers and even curious tourists were awaiting them on the shore. The three were desperate and gratefully accepted an offer for a smaller craft to take them to a little inlet farther down the coast and away from the enemy. They no sooner set foot on the little ship when they realized they were tricked. On board were the dreaded press and photographers who had their victims cornered and ghoulishly tortured the trio with their questions and demands for "special" camera shots. The horror of that experience remained an open wound that never healed and never left Mr. B.

Another hurt he could never handle was the persistent rumor that he actually did not write his music. The gossip around town was that he had "a little black boy who composed all of his songs". Utter rubbish! Before *This Is The Army* left England to join the troops in Italy, Mr. B called me to his room and he played a song he had just written for the 5th Army stationed there. I'm afraid I wasn't too responsive and he quickly volunteered, "You're probably right, it lacks something, it won't do." A half-hour later, he called me again. Once more he played another song he had just finished, and once more, "It's still not right." This went on two more times and finally he announced, "This is it! ... It's right ... I feel it," and a spirited marching song was dedicated to the 5th Army. Mr. B had composed all that music within a three hour span and there was no "little black boy" in sight.

Cole Porter was once asked to name one of his favorite songs – apart from his own, of course. His immediate answer was Irving Berlin's *All Alone*. He explained how the title *All Alone* sets an immediate mood: the first sixteen bars of the haunting melody and the accompanying lyric are a complete song in themselves and enchant the listener:

All alone, I'm so all alone

There is no-one else but you

All alone by the telephone

Waiting for a ring, a ting-aling

175

The song captures the essence of loneliness and most everyone can relate to that.

The celebrated actress Helen Hayes told a beautifully poignant story about one of Irving Berlin's songs and the very special meaning it had for her. Her friends were very concerned about her relationship with Charles MacArthur, the writer. His reputation was questionable, he drank too much, he was a philanderer, and they worried he would ruin her career. But the lady was desperately in love. One night when the two were aimlessly roaming on Broadway, they turned onto West 44th Street and as they passed the Irving Berlin Music Building they could see the lights were on, which meant Irving (she called him that) was still working. They no sooner began their sad story when Mr. B interrupted and insisted they listen to a song he had just written. That song, *Always*, had the answer to their problems: "I'll be loving you always, with a love that's true, always." And every year after that on the MacArthurs' wedding anniversary, no matter where they were, the lovers would reach for the other's hand and quietly sing to each other, "I'll be loving you always."

Irving Berlin's music reached everyone, the most sophisticated and the very naïve. His melodies were uncomplicated, the lyrics were honest, and the tune could be hummed after hearing it for the first time. That format worked for him and he produced hit after hit. He never bothered about comparisons. He was modest up to a point, yet he would gladly sing one of his new tunes to anyone who would listen. He really didn't sing, he whispered his songs.

Irving Berlin was a very generous man who donated the royalties from several of his most successful songs to worthwhile charities. This feisty bundle of boundless energy would go without sleep until the job was done, which made it difficult for him because he was a perfectionist who never neglected the slightest detail. He was as concerned with *This Is The Army* troops traveling all over war-torn Europe as he was with his important films, *Holiday Inn* and *White Christmas*. In fact, whenever there was a break in production at the studios, he would rush to rejoin our company, ignoring air raids and shellings, no matter what or where, just to be sure the show was in good shape. He had very deep feeling for people. Once, on a return to the States, he took it upon himself, busy as he was, to phone every parent of the 150 men in our outfit to assure them that their loved ones were well and in good spirits. He was intensely patriotic. He loved America with a fervor very few have. We owe him so much. After all, he gave us our alternative anthem, *God Bless America.*

There aren't enough ways for me to acknowledge and thank the late Irving Berlin for his most extraordinary gift to me – my career. A career which spans some sixty-odd years working exclusively in the entertainment industry. An industry populated by artisans, stage crews, technicians, performers and creative artists, all working together to produce entertainment that would satisfy audiences wherever they may be.

There's a very strong camaraderie among people who work in the entertainment industry. There are very few strangers – only friends. In fact, the first time I worked with one of the superstars, I was very apprehensive because I thought that they were untouchable. Not so. I merely found that we were on an equal footing. In fact, some of those icons have since become some of my closest friends.

It's a magical world, the world of entertainment. Where the unreal suddenly becomes real. And values that you thought were most important in life have little significance when you are busy creating, giving life to an idea or an expression that will mean so much to the real world we live in. I was very privileged to belong to that world of entertainment. The best part of my life was spent working with these wonderful, sometimes eccentric, sometimes magical, people. The rewards were great – wonderful memories that I have of my life in the business.

Now that I am retired and am much, much older, I have the luxury of those memories when I am alone to comfort and sustain me while time races by. Irving Berlin was so right when he wrote, "there's no business like show business."

Robert Sidney

Index

Printed in the United States
1300500007B/76-111